Jennifer Day is a qualified stress management consultant and counselor with many years' experience in the performing arts as a teacher, producer and choreographer. She is also a mother and has run popular creative workshops for children in the United Kingdom and Europe. She currently lives and works in Hawaii, where she runs workshops for children, parents and teachers, based on the concepts contained in this book.

Creative Visualization with Children

A PRACTICAL GUIDE

Jennifer Day

ELEMENT

Shaftesbury, Dorset ● Boston, Massachusetts
Melbourne, Victoria

© Element Books Limited 1994
Text © Jennifer Day 1994

Published in Great Britain in 1994 by
Element Books Limited
Shaftesbury, Dorset SP7 8BP

Published in the USA in 1994 by
Element Books, Inc.
160 North Washington Street, Boston , MA 02114

Published in Australia in 1994 by
Element Books and distributed by
Penguin Australia Limited
487 Maroondah Highway, Ringwood, Victoria 3134

Reprinted 1995
Reprinted 1997
Reprinted 1999

Cover illustration by Shella Fairbrother
Cover design by Max Fairbrother
Illustrations by Tammy Day
Design by Roger Lightfoot
Typeset by ROM Data, Falmouth, Cornwall
Printed and bound in Great Britain by
Redwood Books, Trowbridge, Wiltshire

British Library Cataloguing in Publication
data available

Library of Congress Cataloging in Publication
data available

Day, Jennifer
  Creative Visualization with Children, a practical guide/
Jennifer Day
    p. cm.
  ISBN 1-85230-469-3: s10.95
  1. Child rearing. 2. Visualization. 3. Creative ability. 4. Self esteem.
I. Title.
HO769.D32 1994
649.1—dc20   94-26025
                                                       CIP

ISBN 1-85230-469-3

To Tammy

Contents

Acknowledgements

I would like to thank the following without whom this book would never have been written: All the children I have ever taught – especially Adam, Jodie, Emma, Maria, Sophie, Kathy and Tammy – thank you for all our heartfelt moments and for giving me the courage to write this book. Deborah Rozman, thank you for being such a limitless and generous source of inspiration and knowledge – your dedicated pioneerwork with children has cast a bright light for all of us to follow. Stephanie Herzog, thank you for sharing your knowledge and experience so generously. Everyone at the Institute of HeartMath in California, thank you for bringing the heart into such focus and for your truly inspirational research. The Holistic Education Network in England, thank you for your invaluable support. My publisher Michael Mann a special thank you for your faith. Editor John Baldock, thank you for your inestimable guidance. Shakti Gawain, thank you for your support and kind words. Most of all my daughter Tammy, thank you for your beautiful illustrations and for being my greatest joy, inspiration and teacher.

Jennifer Day

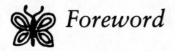 # Foreword

In my years of teaching creative visualization, many people have asked me about how to use this powerful tool most effectively with children. Now Jennifer Day has created a wonderful guidebook for doing exactly that.

Creative Visualization with Children provides clear and practical steps that are easy to understand and follow. Children of all ages, as well as their parents and teachers, will find the exercises helpful, fun and inspiring.

If you would like to guide your children or students in how to use their imaginations to help them learn, develop different aspects of themselves, solve problems, and attain goals, I recommend this book.

Shakti Gawain
Author of *Creative Visualization*

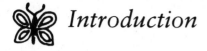 *Introduction*

Creative visualization was recently described to me by an eight-year old as '. . . . the force'. When I asked him to elaborate, he said '. . . . making the imagination become a *force* that can make everything in life better!'

I believe there are many adults who would agree with him. More and more people benefit from creative visualization in all areas of their lives, every day. Artists, athletes, business people, health practitioners, educators and many others are applying it successfully to their professions, health and personal development. Whether using creative visualization or other instruments of personal growth, guidance and help is readily available. Books, articles, courses, workshops, retreats, teachers and gurus are numerous – and on the increase.

As we pursue our own personal development in whatever area of self-help we choose, our children observe us and are often profoundly affected by the changes they see. Their experiences – not only of the rippling effects of change within their families, but also of the constant state of flux within our society and indeed throughout the world today – are unique. No generation has ever grown up surrounded by such perpetual and profound change. Yet there is little help and guidance available for these *children* of our swiftly developing age!

Pathways of guidance and assistance for this young generation are needed. Without such pathways for them to follow, our children may well reach adulthood with a need for as much healing and curative work – emotionally and psychologically – as we ourselves are experiencing.

Although most parents willingly recognize that such guidance is needed, the inevitable question is usually: How can we give guidance to our children when we ourselves are in a continuous state of learning?

Ironically, it is often just when we are growing and learning the most that we can be the very best teachers and guides for our children. This unequivocal truth becomes even clearer when we view the guidance itself in a preventative light.

Consider for a moment the onion. It begins life as a seed. As it grows it gradually develops layers of skin, one layer after another, each layer making it harder to get to the core.

Just like the onion, we humans also gradually develop layers. For us each layer consists of blocks, attitudes and concepts accumulated as we make our way through life. As with the onion, each layer makes it harder to reach the core of our being.

Now increasingly many of us are attempting to peel off these layers as we seek to re-connect with our core selves and with our 'inner child'. This can be as tearful a process as peeling an onion – though usually somewhat more traumatic! Given the conscious choice, the process of peeling is not one most of us would wish for our children. However, as we ourselves become more aware, we increase our ability as parents to provide preventative measures. Although we do know that a certain amount of 'peeling' or 'un-doing' is inevitable in any young adult seeking independence, we must also recognize that it does not need to be traumatic. If sound and loving guidance has been given in childhood, and the young adult is centered in him or her self – carrying the inner sense of security and knowing that this brings – the process can be illuminating and good to them – not just good *for* them!

Bearing this in mind we view the guidance of our children as a preventative as well as an evolutionary process. By drawing on our own experiences of 'layering' and 'peeling' we can appreciate the need for preventative work. We can also understand what powerful processes are called for to build and develop our children's inner strength and knowing.

Through being aware of our own sense of wonder at self-discovery, we can then guide and inspire our children to discover and expand their own inner world. We can, through connecting with our personal inner child, connect with our own children on many levels, and truly experience their immense potential for glorious evolutionary growth.

Once we explore these areas of ourselves – and creative visualization is a powerful tool for doing so – we soon arrive at the realization that we *can* guide our children along their pathways of personal inner growth and that giving them this guidance can give a new dimension to our experience of parenting.

Along with this realization, frequently comes the added insight that creative visualization is both a natural and an ideal way to facilitate the guidance of children. This insight often comes as a direct result of using creative visualization to explore our own inner child!

So what exactly is creative visualization?

Creative visualization is the conscious use of the creative imagination applied actively in your day-to-day living for the purpose of attaining goals, overcoming obstacles, increasing self-awareness and enhancing the overall quality of your life. In the case of creative visualization as it is used in this book, the purpose is of course to improve and enhance the quality of life for your children and for their future – although you will also undoubtedly experience many benefits yourself!

Using creative visualization with children is especially rewarding as it is usually near to second nature for them. Children have both a natural need and an ability for creative and imaginative play that makes the consciously applied use of imagery almost effortless for them. It certainly makes more sense to most children than many other things they are taught!

Being such a natural tool for children, creative visualization can easily help them to grow up far more aware and centered than they otherwise would. Using various techniques of visualization, we can guide our children in such a way that they retain their natural innate connection with their creative and spiritual selves. Creative visualization can help us show our children how to nurture and cherish their own inner child. Through this we contribute, not only to the growth but to the blossoming of self-assured, intuitive, creative and loving individuals – the kind of individuals that we ourselves are seeking to become.

For children with particular needs or challenges – such as excessive nightmares, irrational fears, over sensitivity, hyperactivity or an inability to concentrate – creative visualization can be an invaluable and indispensable tool for them to overcome or meet their challenges.

Most importantly, through the use of creative visualization the processes of personal inner growth become FUN! Creative visualization will help your children to grow and blossom, *enjoyably* and harmoniously into the fulfilment of their very own individual potential.

This book outlines a series of basic, effective ways for you to use creative visualization with your children. You can use these processes with one child, with your family or even with a play group or in a school situation. In my experience the processes in this book can be used successfully with groups ranging in size from two to twenty.

The simple techniques, principles and ideas are based on my own twenty years of experience working with and teaching children and teenagers throughout the world – and raising my own daughter. They are easy to implement and will help develop your children's creativity, self-esteem, focus and concentration, increase their awareness and self-mastery and give them a stabilizing sense of centeredness so vital for children growing up in the tumultuous nineties.

This book can be used by all parents and guardians, whether you are new to creative visualization or you are already familiar with and practicing forms of self-development, meditation or creative visualization.

Have fun and enjoy!

 PART ONE

Structuring a Session

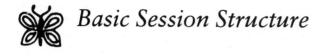

Basic Session Structure

As with most things in life, some structure is needed for a session of creative visualization. Although it is equally important to maintain individual creative freedom, a basic structure is necessary as a frame within which to be creative and stay focused. In my experience the *order* of the processes used in a session of creative visualization is the most important aspect of the structure, as it plays a fundamental part in determining energy levels, energy flows, openness, receptivity and balance.

That being said, the following order does leave room for adjustments and experimentation as you discover and work through your child's – and your own – particular needs. Generally it is advisable to use this order as the basic structural *guideline* and with it create and establish a sense of continuity.

The time periods given are based on a ninety-minute session duration. As this may differ in any given case, these times are intended to be used as a guideline and adjusted according to your individual sessions.

1. *Releasing Restrictions*: Approximately 5 minutes should be spent on this at the beginning of any session. This is important for the release of any tension that might block or disrupt the remainder of the session or any of the processes.

2. *Creative Movement or Kino Visualization*: 10–15 minutes can be spent on one of these. Whichever form you choose, stay with the same one for three or four sessions at least – or until your child is familiar and comfortable with the basic concepts – before moving on to another form. You can of course stay with one form indefinitely if your child really enjoys it!

3. *Breathing*: Approximately 5 minutes of deep abdominal breathing and other breathing exercises is advisable to increase the flow of energy and focus the attention.
4. *Meditation and Centering*: Up to 10 minutes can be given to this process of centering the awareness and focusing energy, depending on the needs and attention span of your child.
5. *Creative Visualization*: A 10 minute process added onto the centering or meditation is recommended. This can be extended depending on the attention span and needs of your child. The creative visualization can be chosen from any one of the following chapters: Creating A Garden, Self-Mastery, Problem Solving, Goal Setting, Friends and Family, Global Awareness or Creative Activity Visualizations.
6. *Creative Activity*: 20–30 minutes can be given to this, including a brief cleaning up if necessary!
7. *Sharing*: 10 minutes is a good time for this, but it will depend very much on the number of people participating.
8. *Outflowing*: To conclude the session, a simple exercise for expanding awareness can take approximately 4 or 5 minutes.

Maintaining a balanced pace within the session is important. Be aware of your child's attention span and energy level and try to pace accordingly. Whereas the centering process is introspective, during an active process the energy is directed outward. Although your child is not necessarily aware of this pattern, it can become a foundation for balance in his or her life and future. It is therefore essential that you are aware of maintaining such a balance.

Be aware also of your child's or children's energies. Flexibility and adaptability cannot be emphasized strongly enough. The energies of your child or children will continuously change – this is particularly true amongst teenagers. It is important to be sensitive to these changes and to be able to adjust or modify your session to suit, without losing the focus and purpose of the session.

Further on in this book you will find chapters on each

section of a session, with a variety of processes from which you can choose and compile your sessions. I suggest that you read through them all – and even try some of the processes by yourself – before you make your choice and attempt them with your child.

On the following pages I give an example of a session that you can use – if you wish – as a 'model' until you begin to put together your own sessions from the subsequent chapters.

Please do not view this session or the outlines and the processes in this book as *fait accompli*, but rather as a basis from which to build, create and grow, together with your child.

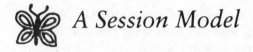 # A Session Model

Before you begin, be sure you have plenty of space and that your space is well ventilated, well lit and has a comfortable temperature. Be sure you are both (or all) wearing loose and comfortable clothing with no restrictive belts or the like. Finally make sure you will not be disturbed for the next 90 minutes or so.

Releasing Restrictions

Put on a tape of percussion or primitive drumming. Now keep in time with the rhythm as you stomp into the floor with one foot at a time. Keep your knees slightly bent and relaxed. Keep doing this, imagining that all your tension is running out of your feet and into the ground. Shake your hands and arms as well, imagining all your stress and tension being shaken out of your body. Keep re-enforcing this to your child – each time you think it, say it! Keep shaking until your whole body is shaking in a heavy and relaxed manner – including your head! Feel free to let out a few shrieks if you feel like it.

Now that all your tension has been shaken out, take a few deep breaths and stand quietly with your feet hip-width apart, arms relaxed alongside your body. Replace the drumming with some quiet melodic music. Ask your child to imagine that the soles of his or her feet have roots that are growing into the earth. Imagine that your body is a long supple tree with your ankle being the joint that you move or sway from. (Sometimes it may help to have your child or children close their eyes to really 'feel' like a tree.) Now ask your child to lean forward as far as they can, as if being gently blown by a soft breeze. Ask them to try not to lift their heels and to keep the knees relaxed. Then ask them to return to the central position and lean to one side – then to the other side, each time as far as possible without lifting the heels, or destroying the roots of the tree! Finally, ask them to lean back as far as possible.

Now, ask them to try to notice exactly where they feel any tension when they lean – and how much of that do they need to stand or to move? Ask them to try to find at what point the tree is the most stable. Where do they have the perfect balance without holding tension in the shoulders, neck, legs or feet? Have them sway for a while until they have found this perfectly balanced position. As soon as they have found it, ask them to keep their eyes closed and to stand perfectly still for a moment, enjoying their own personal position of perfect balance.

Take a few deep breaths together and prepare the music for Creative Movement or Kino Visualization.

Creative Movement

Stretching: Both (or all) of you sit on the floor facing each other. Cross your legs and take a deep breath in. As you breathe out reach slowly forward with outstretched arms until your hands are on the floor. Breathe in and out deeply several times. Each time you breathe out try to reach a little further forward. Imagine that something you want is just a few inches in front of you. Now reach for it! Slowly breathe in and sit up as you breathe out.

Sit with your spines straight, legs crossed and arms lightly resting on your knees. Keeping your elbows stretched slowly make outward circles with your wrists, letting your hands make a full circle. Do this three times outward and three times inward. Imagine you are stirring something really gooey like glue or syrup. Then shake your hands vigorously (shaking off the gooey substance) and relax.

Stretch your legs out in front of you and take a deep breath in. As you breathe out, slowly reach forward letting the weight of your head carry it towards your knees. Keep breathing easily and evenly. Keep your shoulders and neck relaxed and don't forget to remind your child to do the same! Keep reaching, feeling the pull of gravity until you can give your knees a great big kiss! Breathe out slowly as you sit up. Repeat.

Relax!

Improvised Dance

Play a tape of the music of your choice – just be sure that you and your child agree on the style of music you are playing. Sit quietly and listen to the music for a few minutes – preferably with your eyes closed. As soon as you feel familiar with the music, begin to move gradually. You can open your eyes now! Gently encourage your child – and yourself – to dance freely to the music, expressing exactly what you feel, as if the music is playing *through* you. You can dance apart or together, side by side or back to back – whichever way you both feel most comfortable with. Enjoy!

Breathing

Sit in a comfortable position, either on the edge of a cushion on the floor or on a chair. Make sure that your spines are straight and your limbs are relaxed.

Begin by focusing on the breath. Ask your child to place both hands lightly on the stomach. Now ask him or her to breathe in, letting the chest and stomach expand. Relax the mouth and jaw as you breathe so that the air can get right down to the base of the lungs. Ask your child to try to feel the entire abdomen expand and fill with air. Then let it out *gradually*, starting from the abdomen, until all the air has been expelled. Repeat. (It may take a little time to connect the breath with the lower abdomen to begin with. With patience the connection will be made!)

Having repeated this breathing exercise about ten times, have your child just breathe evenly and naturally for a few minutes, focusing their attention on their own natural breath.

Centering/Meditating

Have your child continue to breathe evenly and naturally and focus on a point in front of him or her and slightly upwards. As they focus on this point, suggest that they may be feeling their eyelids becoming heavier. Tell them to close their eyes as soon as it feels natural (it will, as long as they keep focused on the point in front of them!) Read the following 'script' to your child making sure your voice is calm, soft and audible. Try not to sound monotonous and pause regularly so that all you say may be absorbed.

Gently place your hand on your heart and listen for your heartbeat. Feel the rhythm – is it slowing down or is it even?. . . Keep all your attention on your heart. If other thoughts enter your head, just let them float on by like petals on a river and bring your attention right back to your heart. Now, holding your attention there, think of something or someone that you love – (*you may here mention a pet or a favorite toy, animal or place that you know is special to your child*) – maybe a hug or a puppy – feel what that thought does to your heart. . . . how does that make you feel? Does the area of your heart feel different. . . . nicer maybe?. . . . Hold that loving feeling in your heart for a little while, really hold on to it. Enjoy how nice it feels. . . .

Be quiet for a few minutes or as long as your child's attention span is capable of. At this point you may want to begin *very softly* playing a tape of relaxation music and turning up the volume very gradually, but never so it distracts from your voice. This is the appropriate time to continue on and intro-duce the creative visualization.

Creative Visualization

Maintain your calm and audible voice throughout this process, not forgetting to take pauses.

Now I want you to see before you a path in nature. . . . any way you want it to be. . . . wide, narrow, winding, straight, by a stream or by the sea, in a forest or in the mountains. . . . whatever you like. . . . Now I want you to walk down your path until you come to a tree, a tree with many branches. This is your Trouble Tree, the tree where you hang all your troubles. Pause for a moment and offload all your troubles – no matter how small. Hang them all on the tree before you move on. . . . Now continue on down your path. If there are any rocks or twigs or other obstacles, stop and gently move them to the side. Give them some of all that love you have in your heart and move on. Soon you arrive at a small gate covered in your favorite flowers. Smell their lovely fragrance as you gently push open the gate. As you step through your gate you enter into the most beautiful garden you have ever seen. It is exactly the way you want it to be and it is all your very own. . . . All the colors in your garden are very bright and beautiful. The sun is shining, the birds are singing a welcoming song and you feel very safe and peaceful here. . . . Wander through your garden for a while, exploring. . . . *(pause for a few moments or for as long as your child's attention span holds)*. . . . Now before you leave, I want to you to thank your garden for being there for you and for being so perfect. Know that your garden will *always* be there for you whenever you need it. . . . *(If you have been playing music in the background, you can now begin to slowly turn down the volume as you speak until the music is almost inaudible. As you near the end of the process, slightly speed up your rate of speech and turn the volume on the music right down.)* Now gradually bring your attention back to your heart again. . . . Has your heartbeat changed at all? Feel the love inside your heart and send it all around your body. . . . Feel the nice sensation of love everywhere. . . . Now bring your attention to your breathing. Has it slowed down? Now very gradually bring your attention back into this room. . . . and when you are ready you can open your eyes knowing that *(mention whatever activity you have chosen)* is going to be lots of fun and we are really going to enjoy it and benefit from it!

Creative Activity

If you have not chosen an activity I suggest you draw or write – whatever comes easiest to you both. Draw or write *whatever comes to you*. It does not have to make sense to you at the moment. Please emphasize this to your child. He or she can draw or write *anything they want*. I have found this most beneficial when children know that they do not have to show their drawing or writing to you if they do not want to. Do not try to cajole them into showing it to you. It is private – just like yours!

Sharing

When you have finished your activity, sharing can be very valuable as long as both or all involved want to share and no judgement or comment is passed on what is shared.

Heart to heart sharing: This is ideal for two people. When sharing heart to heart, one person speaks – sharing an experience in as much detail as possible (for example, their 'garden', or 'path') while the other person listens, all the time feeling love in their heart and sending love from their heart to the heart of the speaker. When the sharing is complete, the listener repeats – in his or her own words – all that has been shared. The person who shared verifies or adds if necessary. When this is concluded, change roles and repeat the process. Try throughout to retain the feeling of love in the heart.

Outflowing

Sit comfortably and close your eyes. Lead your child through this or pre-record it on your tape player and do it together!

Now take a few deep breaths until you feel very relaxed and comfortable. . . . Now take a deep breath and feel the energy of the universe (*you can say 'of God' or 'of universal love' here – whatever feels most comfortable to you*) through the crown of your head. Feel it going down to your heart and filling your heart with love. . . . Now release it out into the world, through your heart. Breathe in again, breathing in universal love and energy through the crown of your head and out through your heart. Again . . . breathe in universal love, energy and wisdom . . . in through the crown of your head and out through your heart. . . . Feel your body filling up with universal love . . . feel the space around you filling up with universal love. . . . As you breathe in and out, feel the whole room fill up with universal love . . . feel the entire building fill up with universal love, energy and wisdom. . . . Breathe in and out and feel the area around your house filling up with universal love . . . feel the town filling up . . . the state . . . the entire country, filled with universal love, energy and wisdom. Breathe in through the crown of your head and out through your heart and feel the entire world fill with universal love . . . feel it spreading across the whole globe. Now feel it completely filling the whole universe . . . feel the love, energy and wisdom everywhere. . . . Now bring your attention back to your breathing . . . feel the slow relaxed rhythm of your breathing blending together with everyone else in this room. . . . Become aware of the room around you . . . and when you are ready you can open your eyes . . .

It is always nice to end the session with a great big hug!

 PART TWO

Preparation

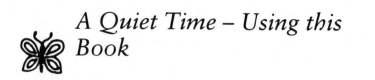

A Quiet Time – Using this Book

It is a good idea to establish a set 'quiet time' – a time for creative visualization and centering – on a regular basis, preferably at the same time each week or even every day if you can. Should anything cause the cancellation of your quiet time, try to re-schedule it immediately, as you would with any other important family routine.

As I suggested earlier, before you begin to use this book, give yourself some time to go through it alone. That way you will become familiar with the outlined processes before attempting them with your child. It is important that you participate fully in your quiet time with your child or children and that they do not feel lectured or 'read to'. Don't be afraid to let your child know that you are learning and growing too and that your quiet time together is for mutual benefit and enjoyment. Use it to better understand each other as well as yourselves.

You can use this book with all age groups, from three-year olds to young adults. You may like to use it with your entire family together, or do a separate session for the younger members, if appropriate. As you progress you will discover that you can also adapt the outlined processes to the different age groups. Feel free to experiment as you become more familiar with the various processes. Eventually you may wish to develop your own – more personally suited to the individual needs of your children and yourself.

Gradually you will find yourself using creative visualization for many areas of your and your children's lives, and at many times of the day – not just during your quiet time. Eventually it will become a natural part of your everyday lives.

As with most things, creative visualization takes regular practice and upkeep. It is therefore important that your quiet time is established as a regular routine and given priority in your lives, no matter how busy or preoccupied you become. Usually it is when we are at our busiest and most preoccupied that we need that quiet time the most!

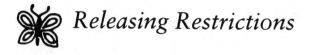

Releasing Restrictions

At the beginning of any quiet or special time with your child and before you do anything else, it is important to remove any restrictions that might block or disrupt the process and your time together.

Restrictions can take several forms;

1. *Space*: Make sure you are in a room that is warm and comfortable and has ample floor space for you to move about on. Be sure you and your child can swing your arms about without the fear of breaking anything.
2. *Clothing*: Take your shoes off and insure that any restrictive pieces of clothing – such as belts and tight jeans – are removed.
3. *Noise*: Be sure you have turned on the answering machine or unplugged the phone. If you fear you might be interrupted by someone at your front door, put a note on the door saying you are not to be disturbed.
4. *Mental*: If either you or your child is exceptionally tired, leave your creative visualization and quiet time for later, or another day. If however your child is not tired but merely 'doesn't feel like it', kindly but firmly tell him or her that this is your special time together and remind them how it makes them feel. This will usually do the trick. If your child still insists on not doing it, calmly give them the option of spending the time in his or her room – on no account disturbing you – while you close the door and have the special quiet time to yourself (or with your other children). Under no circumstances must you cancel it. You will soon find that your child will wish to join in again.
5. *Physical*: These restrictions usually take the form of physical

tension such as tense shoulders, neck, arms and buttocks, caused by stress. Following are some tension-release exercises you can do together that will relieve stress reactions and enhance the flow of energy. Until you have memorized them, it is advisable to pre-record the instructions on tape and play it back. That way, you will not be distracted by having to constantly refer to these pages.

Tense and Let Go

Stand facing each other, in a circle if you are more than two. Have everyone lift their right leg slightly off the floor and tense all the muscles in the leg until it begins to vibrate. At the count of three relax the leg, making it go limp. Repeat with the left leg. Now tense the stomach, buttocks and pelvic area, as tight as possible. Exaggeration can often make this more fun for children! At the count of three relax, letting the stomach 'hang out'. Repeat with the back and chest area. Now hold the right arm to the front and tense all the muscles in the arm until it begins to vibrate. Clench the fist and bend the elbow, flexing the upper arm muscles and simulating a body-builder (Popeye, for example). At the count of three relax, letting the arm hang limply at your side. Repeat with the left arm. Now lift the shoulders and tense the neck as much as possible. Again, exaggerate. Relax, drawing attention to how different the shoulders and neck feel when they are not tense. Now clench the teeth and tense the jaw, followed by the facial muscles. Squeeze the eyes tightly shut, frown hard and tense the entire scalp. Enjoy the funny faces you all make! At the count of three relax, ensuring that the jaw and tiny muscles around the eyes also relax. Now bend forward and 'hang' limply with your arms dangling towards the floor for a minute or so, letting any remaining excess tension run out of your arms, through your fingers and into the floor.

Shakin'

Play a tape of primitive drums or percussion (see the recommended music list at the back of this book). Keeping in time with the rhythm, stomp into the ground or floor with one foot at a time, keeping your knees bent and relaxed. Keep on stomping, imagining that you are barefoot in the sand or earth and that with each stomp you are creating a deep foot-print. Start shaking your arms and hands at the same time, as if shaking off water. Now feel your neck completely loose and shake your head gently. As you do this, inhibitions will gradually be released and you will soon be shaking wildly! Feel free to let out a few primal shrieks as well.

Be a Tree

Stand with your feet hip-width apart, arms relaxed alongside the body. Imagine that the soles of your feet have roots, growing through the floor and into the earth. Imagine that your body is a long, supple tree with your ankle being the joint that you move or sway from. Now lean forward as far as you can, as if being blown by a gentle breeze. Try not to lift your heels. You may want to relax your knees slightly. Return to the central position and lean to one side and then the other, each time as far as you can without lifting your feet (or destroying your roots!). Finally, lean back as far as you can. Notice where you feel tension as you lean – how much of that do you need to stand or to move? Try to find at what point your tree is the most stable – where you have perfect balance without holding unnecessary tension in your shoulders, neck, calves or feet. As soon as you have located the position, close your eyes and stand perfectly still for a moment, enjoying your own personal position of minimal stress.

You and your children can remind each other of this whenever you observe physical tension in each other. 'Being a Tree' is a quick way to check for tension during the course of the day and you may be surprised at how astute your child is at recognizing when *you* are holding tension!

Re-energize!

Rub your hands together vigorously. Shake them hard and then squeeze each finger and pull it away from you. Shake your hands again until they are warm and your fingers tingle. Make a fist and keep loose in the wrist, as if you are about to knock on a door. Now lightly tap the top of the head and brow with the knuckles. It can be fun for smaller children to tell their brain cells to 'wake up!' as they do this.

Cup the left elbow in the right hand and pound the top of the right shoulder with the fist of the left hand. Pound from the neck out to the shoulder and back. Change hands and repeat on the other shoulder. Now stretch both arms up towards the sun and take a deep breath in. With light and loose fists, pound chest as you let all the air out of your lungs with a long, loud 'Tarzan' shriek!

Have your child bend forward – or if you are more than two, split into pairs and have one person bend forward – placing their hands lightly on their knees, forming a table-top with their back. Stand behind your child and with loose fists lightly tap alongside both sides of the spine, from the neck all the way down and back up again. It is vital that the actual spine is *not* tapped at all. Change places and repeat. (Should you be too tall for your child to reach, bend your knees or go down on all fours!)

Finally a non-physical tension-release exercise for the days when some 'mental house cleaning' is called for!

Erase Erase!

Place a large basket in the center of the room. Give everyone a sheet of paper and a pencil. Now take five minutes – in silence – to each write down as many words of anger, negative thoughts and other expressions of frustration that each one of you can think of. Keep it completely confidential! When everyone has finished, tear your sheets of paper up in as many small pieces as possible, each person keeping their own pieces of paper. Holding onto the torn pieces each person holds their hands over the basket. Now all together in unison say: ERASE! ERASE! ERASE! ERASE! – LOVING THOUGHTS WILL TAKE THEIR PLACE! As the word 'place' is said, everyone throws their torn pieces of paper into the basket. The basket should then be removed as everyone takes a moment to focus on loving thoughts.

Creative Movement

Having released restrictions and stress, it is important – particularly for children – to channel the energy and focus the awareness. Certain forms of physical exercise and creative movement can be ideal for this purpose, placing your body in the best possible state for meditation and creative visualization.

One such form that is *particularly* helpful in preparing for creative visualization is Image-Body movement or Kino Visualization. It is, briefly, movements performed by the physical body and the image body (the non-physical body) separately and simultaneously. This is explained and explored in detail in the next chapter.

Other appropriate forms of creative movement and exercise are Yoga, Stretching, Isometric exercise and various types of dancing.

YOGA

Following are a few simple, basic yoga exercises that are ideal for children and families.

The Snake: Lie on your stomach with the palms of your hands face down by your shoulders, elbows on the floor. Take a deep breath in and lift up your chest until your elbows are straight. With smaller children it can be fun to stick out the tongue like a snake at this point! Try to keep the shoulders down and the pelvic area firmly on the floor. As you bend your elbows and lower your chest to the floor again, let out a long hiss like a snake. Then relax for a moment and let the snake rest. Repeat.

Figure 1. The Snake

The Cat: Kneel with your hands on the floor in front of you, elbows straight. Arch the back like a cat as far as you can letting your head and shoulders round. Hiss like a cat if you like! Now release the back, dropping it to curve as far as possible, head and chest lifted. Purr like a cat! Repeat.

Figure 2. The Cat

The Dog: Lie on your stomach with the palms of your hands face down by your waist. Your legs should be a little more than hip-width apart, toes tucked under and pressed into the floor, heels up! Breathe in and push up with your hands and feet until your body forms an upside down V-shape. Push your heels into the ground and drop your head in line with your back, breathing out. Growl like a dog! Return to the floor and rest. Repeat.

Figure 3. The Dog

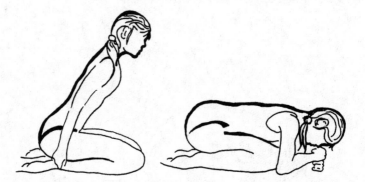

Figure 4. The Bunny Rabbit

The Bunny Rabbit: Kneel on the floor sitting on your heels. Take a deep breath in and lift the chest, stretching the spine upwards and forwards. Continue the movement forwards breathing out as you bend over. Keep stretching until your chest rests on your thighs. Place one fist on top of the other on the floor in front of you and rest your forehead on them. Let the bunny rabbit sleep! Breathe in, lift the head and slowly return to the seated position, breathing out. Repeat.

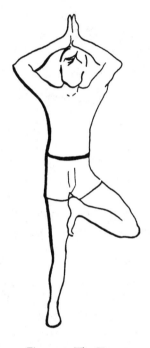

Figure 5. The Tree

The Tree: Stand straight with your feet together. Identify a point on the wall in front of you. Be sure it is a still point. Concentrate your attention on the point. This will help you to keep your balance! Now lift your left foot and place it just above your right knee, keeping the left knee facing out to the side. Lift your arms slowly above your head bringing the palms of the hands together. Breathe in and out slowly. Stretch your arms a little higher and press your shoulders down. Breathe in and out again. Feel the calm sensation of being a firm and sturdy oak tree. Breathe in and as you breathe out slowly lower your arms and leg. Repeat with the other leg.

The Corpse: Lie flat on your back with your legs a little more than hip-width apart and the ankles and feet relaxed. Turn the arms out from the shoulders, hands away from your sides, palms facing upwards. Close your eyes and relax completely, imagining that you are a corpse. Try to really feel what it is like to be a corpse, completely still!

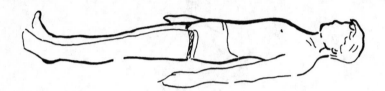

Figure 6. The Corpse

STRETCHING

Following are some simple stretching exercises designed for all ages. Do them in the order that they are listed.

Exercise 1:   Sit on the floor with your legs crossed as in Figure 7. Breathe in deeply. As you breathe out reach forward slowly with both your arms stretched in front of you until your hands are on the floor. Breathe in and out deeply several times. Each time you breathe out, reach a little further forward. Imagine a special treat (for example a big chocolate cake!) a few inches in front of you. Reach for it! Now breathe in and sit up as you breathe out. Repeat.

Figure 7.

Exercise 2: Sit with your spine straight, legs crossed and arms resting on your knees as in Figure 7. Keeping your elbows stretched, slowly make outward circles with your wrists (so that your hands make a full circle) three times outward and three times inward. Imagine you are stirring something gooey like glue or syrup. Then shake your hands vigorously (shaking off the gooey substance) and relax.

Exercise 3:   Stretch your legs out in front of you as in Figure
8. Keep your spine straight and relax your arms at your sides.
Imagine you have a piece of rainbow chalk attached to each
big toe, and that you have a blackboard in front of your feet.
Now flex your feet as far as you can, preferably until your heels
no longer touch the floor. 'See' the beautiful line you have
drawn with the chalk! Now turn your legs out from the hip
(keeping your feet flexed) so that your toes face outward,
making a big curve with your chalk. Be sure to keep your knees
stretched! Now point your toes and feet, stretching your legs
as hard as you can. Your little toes should just touch the floor.
Now turn your legs parallel again and repeat. Breathe evenly
throughout.

Exercise 4:   Keeping your legs stretched in front of you as in
Figure 8, slowly reach forward with your hands letting the
weight of the head carry it towards your knees. Breathe
easily and evenly, keeping your shoulders and neck relaxed.
Keep reaching, feeling the pull of gravity until you can kiss
your own knees! Breathe out slowly as you sit up. Repeat.

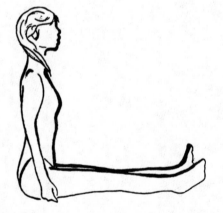

Figure 8.

ISOMETRICS

Isometric movement or exercise is basically when the muscles act against each other or against a fixed object, to increase awareness and improve muscle tone. Following are a few basic isometric exercises for everyone.

Doorway: Stand in a doorway and lift your arms so that the back of each hand touches the door frame. Now press really hard with both hands against the door frame. Keep pressing as hard as you can for the count of ten. Relax. (If you step out of the doorway and let your arms hang loosely alongside you, you will find that your arms will slowly move upwards and away from your body!)

Arms and Legs: Sit on the floor with your knees bent, soles of your feet together and hands resting on your ankles (Figure 9). Keep your back straight and your neck long! Now breathe in and as you breathe out, bend your elbows so that they rest on your knees as you lean forward slightly. Holding onto your ankles, push down on your knees with your elbows. At the same time, push up with your knees. Keep pushing your elbows and knees against each other for a count of ten. Then relax for a count of ten. Repeat. Note which is the stronger, your arms or your legs!

Figure 9.

Squeeze: Lie on your back with a book or a small pillow under your head. Bend your knees, placing the soles of your feet on the floor, hip-width apart. Let your arms rest alongside your body. Place a large, firm pillow between your knees as in Figure 10. (It must be large enough to prevent you from bringing your legs together.) Breathe in deeply and as you breathe out, squeeze the pillow with your knees as hard as you can. Try to lengthen your breath so that you squeeze for a full count of ten. Then relax. Repeat.

Figure 10.

Alligator: Place the palms of your hands together in front of your chest, as if in prayer. Make sure your elbows are straight out to the side and your shoulders are down. Breathe in and as you breathe out press the palms of your hands together as hard as you can. Try to press hard for the count of ten. Then relax, leaving the heels of the hands together while moving the palms and fingers away from each other – opening up like the mouth of an alligator! (See Figure 11.) Repeat.

DANCING

There are many types of dancing you can do to channel and focus your energy. If you and your child are familiar with and

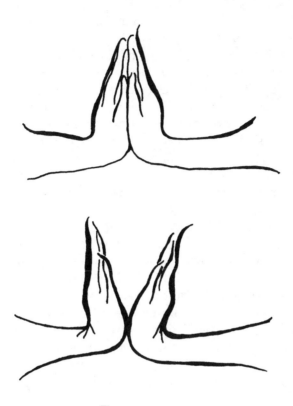

Figure 11.

enjoy a particular style of dancing, it is often a good idea to utilize this option, at least in the first few sessions. Following are some suggested dance forms and uses of dance that are simple to implement and enjoyable for all ages.

Folk Dancing: If you have a basic knowledge of your own indigenous folk dance, this is an opportunity to give your child a sense of it. It is essential that you have the right music so that authenticity, atmosphere and a true feeling for the dance is created. Do the very simplest of steps but do not 'instruct' your child. Just let them follow you, feeling at ease to make mistakes. Guide or correct them only when they request it. Relax and enjoy it!

Improvised Dance: This is a free form of dance, done to the music of your choice. You can use classical music, jazz, music from a musical, new age music or popular music – just be sure that you and your child agree on the style of music to be used. It often helps to listen to the music once before you begin dancing. When you dance, be careful not to focus on or judge each other in any way. This will only inhibit the process. Let the music guide your movements as if it is being played through you. Many children enjoy pretending to dance for an audience of deaf people – showing them what the music sounds like, with their movements! For suggestions of music, see the recommended music list at the back of the book.

Mime Dancing: This combination of silent acting and dance allows you to depict something specific – a character (for example a clown or a juggler) or something in nature (like a growing flower or a bird). Music is also of great help in this process, as it can contribute to the creation of the right atmosphere for your chosen mime (see recommended music list). Having created your characters individually, you may want them to interact (for example, a bird fluttering round a flower or a clown trying to 'help' a juggler). Take your time, use your imagination and have fun with this!

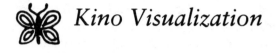 # Kino Visualization

The word Kino is Greek for motion and dynamics, and Hawaiian for body. Together with visualization it depicts body-image movement, movement that is performed by the physical and the image (or subtle) body, separately and simultaneously.

Many people today accept that we have a secondary, subtle (non-physical) body, an etheric image of our own body. Certain members of the medical profession would call it 'the body of muscular imagination'. Teachers of yoga may refer to it as the 'Pranic body'. Whatever you call it, extensive research has discovered that developing awareness and use of this 'image-body' increases movement potential, bodily functions and indeed contributes greatly to the natural healing process.

Having worked with the image-body in the teaching of dance and movement for many years, I have witnessed astounding results both physically and in terms of awareness. Hence image-body work or Kino Visualization has gradually become a separate process and a subject matter unto itself. I have found that children and adolescents in particular derive great enjoyment from this work. It is an added bonus that other benefits can be observed within a reasonably short time – such as increased self-awareness, self-confidence and often greatly improved physical health!

The following are some basic exercises using creative movement in the physical body and the image body. These exercises will help increase the awareness, energy flow and movement abilities, concentrate the body and the attention, focus the imagination in preparation for visualization and create a lot of fun for both you and your children!

Head: Sit up straight with your head facing front, eyes looking straight ahead. Now turn your head slowly to the right, as far as you can and focus on a point in the room as far away from you and as far around to the right as possible. Now bring your head back to face front. Repeat to the left. Now close your eyes and just get a sense of turning your head – don't physically do it – just imagine that you are turning your head slowly, loosely and freely first to the right and then to the left, far around to each side. Now imagine bringing your head back to face front. Open your eyes and once again physically turn your head, first to the right, as far as you can and focus on the point furthest away and furthest to the right. Repeat to the left. What has happened? Most likely your head turned noticeably further to both sides!

Figure 12.

Torso: Stand with your legs a little more than hip-width apart, feet firmly on the ground. Imagine that your spine is a pole and that your torso is going to move around it. Keeping your legs completely still, slowly spiral your shoulders and torso to the right, as far as you can (Figure 12) and then return to the central position. Repeat to the left. Now close your eyes and stand perfectly still, imagining that your shoulders and torso are spiraling freely and easily to the right, returning to the central position with ease and grace and then spiraling freely again to the left. See your body returning to the central position again with easy elegance – this is your image body. Now open your eyes and spiral to the right with your physical torso. Then to the left. Now stand still and 'see' your image-body spiral to the right. Then physically spiral to the right. Now see your image-body spiral to the left followed by your physical body. Note how much easier it is to spiral physically after your image-body has performed a spiral.

Arms: Stand with your legs hip-width apart, feet firmly on the ground. Raise your physical right arm to the front and up over your head (Figure 13). Feel how this affects the muscles throughout your body and the material of the clothes you are wearing. Feel the stretch in your shoulder, arm and hand. Maintaining the same awareness, lower your arm.

Now do the same with your image-body right arm – do not physically lift your arm, just visualize it rising out and up over your head, feeling the influence this has on the rest of your body. Now lower your image-body arm. Repeat everything with the left arm. Then with both arms together.

Legs: Stand with your feet together, arms alongside you. Slowly step forward onto your left foot and be aware of how this affects the muscles in the rest of your body. Feel the

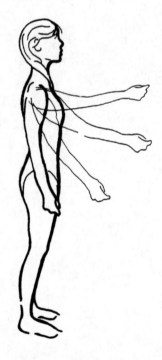

Figure 13.

muscles in your left leg and foot. With the same awareness, step back with your left foot to the starting position. Now do the same with your image-body left leg – not physically! Feel how it affects your entire body. Repeat everything with your right leg. Now bend both legs slightly and make a small jump forward. Stop and notice how your body has reacted. Now jump back with the same awareness. Now make this jump with your image-body, seeing yourself jump with ease and lightness. How does your image-body feel? Repeat everything.

Figure 14.

All Together: Stand with your feet together, arms alongside you. Step forward with your left foot, both arms reaching forward and turning your head to the left (looking over your left shoulder). Stop and be aware of the changes in your muscles. Return to the starting position. Now repeat with your right foot, looking over your right shoulder (Figure 14). Make sure you are equally aware of your muscles. Now do the same with your image-body, first on the left, then on the right side. Maintain your awareness throughout and see yourself move with great ease and grace. Now repeat with your physical body. Repeat with your image-body.

Defying Gravity: Stand with your feet together, knees slightly bent, arms alongside you. Physically jump up in the air, tucking your arms into your chest and your feet up underneath you (try to kick your own buttocks!). When you land, stop and focus your awareness on how your body feels. Now, with your image-body jump as high as you can, tucking your feet under you and your arms into your chest. See yourself jumping really high and effortlessly. Do it again and feel as if you are a ball, bouncing easily, again and again! Now physically jump again, in the same way. See if you aren't jumping higher than you physically were before.

Partners: Stand facing each other (in pairs if you are more than two), feet together and arms alongside you. Be mirrors to each other as you (physically) lift your arms out to the side and up over your heads. Slowly bring them down again, all the while being aware of your partner as you mirror each other. Repeat. Now turn away from each other and 'see' your image-body facing you. Again lift both arms out and up over your heads as you 'see' your image-body do the same. Now slowly lower your arms, mirroring your own image-body as you go. Repeat.

Follow the Leader: Stand with your feet together, arms alongside you. Sense your image-body for a moment. Now, leaving your image-body where it is, take three steps forward. Let your image-body follow, taking three steps to join you. Again, leaving your image-body where it is, take three steps back. Let your image-body follow, taking three steps back. Repeat the same process moving sideways, first to the left and then to the right. Now reverse the process and let your image-body take three steps forward, then follow it with your physical body. Does that feel different? Continue the process until your image-body has led the way in all four directions.

Touching the Stars: Crouch down on the floor and sense your image-body for a moment. Leaving your image-body in the crouched position, stand up and reach for the stars – all the way up on tip-toe. Crouch down again. Now see your image-body stand up and reach for the stars, on tip-toe. See it reach the stars with ease and then crouch gracefully down again. See your image-body reach up again, but this time as soon as it reaches the stars, physically follow it, going into your image-body as you reach further than you have ever reached before, touching the stars!

Skiing: Stand with your legs slightly separated, arms hanging loosely at your sides. Close your eyes, take a deep breath and feel yourself relax. Sense your image-body for a moment. Now make a picture in your mind of a snow-covered mountain. See the white triangular shape of the mountain stand out against a brilliant blue sky. Put yourself (with your image-body) in the picture – transport yourself to the mountain. Feel the crisp, cold air against your cheeks and take another deep breath, drinking in the fresh smell of the clear, pure air. Now imagine yourself wearing a pair of skis (if you can't ski imagine that you can). Now see your image-body set off down the mountain, skiing effortlessly. Then physically bend both knees and lean slightly forward, setting off down the mountain behind your image-body. Gently rock up and down at the knees, letting your arms hang loosely. See your image-body moving gracefully in front of you – it may be swinging the arms in rhythm with the rocking of the legs. Do physically whatever your image-body is doing. As you become more and more graceful and move more and more effortlessly, like your image-body, you begin to go faster. As you move faster and faster down the mountainside, imagine the wind rushing past your face. Keep rocking up and down, swinging your arms as your skis carry you along. . . . until quite effortlessly and naturally you fuse with your image-body and become one. Feel the freedom of whizzing down the mountainside until you are quite breathless. Now gradually slow to a halt. Wasn't that fun?

Dancing: Sit in a comfortable position with your eyes closed and listen to a piece of previously chosen music. Allow the music to flow over you, through you and around you. Imagine the music entering you and as it leaves you, taking your image-body with it. See your image-body dancing in complete harmony with the music. See the movements of your image-body as the perfect expression of the music. See your image-body and the music blending together with ease, grace and total enjoyment. Now play the music again and physically reproduce all your image-body movements, becoming one with the music (with older children it may help to turn down the lights or to dance facing away from them the first few times, should they be self-conscious). Notice how differently you respond to the music after this process!

If you have difficulty following the processes in this chapter from the book, pre-record them and play them back for instructional purposes until you are familiar with the processes. If you do pre-record, be sure to speak slowly and to leave spaces on the tape for the execution of the movements.

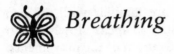 *Breathing*

To take your child into a quiet, relaxed and meditative state, it is necessary for you both to be concentrated, calm and centered. Sitting cross legged on a cushion on the floor is usually the best position to adopt as it is one that can be quite easily held and that keeps the energy focused. The true meditative state has our brain waves operating at a slow enough rate (often called the Alpha state, Beta being the state of totally awake and Theta of asleep), to facilitate effective creative visualization. It is therefore essential that we are as relaxed as is absolutely possible. Deep and focused breathing is the next step to this end, having released tension and energy blocks in the body through the physical exercises and creative movement you have just completed.

To begin focusing of the breathing, it may be helpful if you have previously drawn your child's attention to the breathing of a new-born baby. If there is a baby in your house or in your extended family you may allow your child to place a hand on the baby's tummy. Watch how the baby breathes in a relaxed and natural manner, from the abdomen. Let your child know that this is the way we are all born to breathe!

In addition to doing one of the following breathing exercises with your child, be aware of his or her breathing at all times, if you can. Breathing is influenced greatly by our overall moods; anxiety, nervousness and pain all make us breathe faster. Nevertheless we can in turn influence our moods through our breathing, by becoming aware of and counteracting shallow breathing and hyperventilation. When needed, you can help your child become more centered and calm by gently guiding their breathing rhythm – either by coaxing or by holding them close to you and breathing deeply and slowly yourself. Through this last method you will gradually find your child's breathing rhythm matching yours and eventually normalizing.

Deep Breathing

Seated in a cross-legged position, place both hands lightly on the stomach. To begin with, if your child finds it difficult to connect with the abdomen in this position, begin by lying on your back on the floor. Place a support (such as a book), of about two inches height, under your head. Bend your knees until they point up towards the ceiling and place the soles of your feet flat on the floor, legs hip-width apart.

Breathe in letting your chest and stomach expand, with your mouth relaxed and open so that the air can get right down to the base of your lungs. Feel your entire abdomen expand and fill with air, then let it out, starting from the pelvic area until you feel completely empty. Repeat nine or ten times.

Pre-Centering Breathing

Seated in the cross-legged position or on the edge of a chair, try to maintain a straight and relaxed posture. For the count of three, take a deep breath in through the nostrils, keeping the mouth closed. Try to stay connected to the abdomen as in the Deep Breathing exercise above. Now hold the breath for the count of three. Then gradually let the breath out, through the nostrils, for the count of three until you are completely empty. Now hold that empty feeling for the count of three. Repeat this entire process three times, making sure that the mouth is kept closed.

Alternative Pre-Centering Breathing

Still seated in the same position, gently pinch your nostrils shut using your thumb and forefinger. Lifting up your thumb, slowly breathe in through that nostril for the count of three. Replace the thumb (pinching the nostril shut again) and hold for the count of three. Now lift up the forefinger and breathe out gradually for the count of three. Then immediately breathe in again through that same nostril for the count of three. Replace the forefinger (pinching the nostril shut) and hold for the count of three. Lift up the thumb and breathe out for the count of three. Repeat several times, slowly!

When you have completed one or two of the breathing exercises, focus the attention on your own natural breathing – and of course have your child focus on theirs – for a moment. Encourage your child (and yourself) to breathe deeply, easily and naturally. Pay attention to the rhythm of your breathing – as you become more and more relaxed, does it slow down?

As we focus on our breathing we become more centered within ourselves. Following this we begin the process of entering into an even more relaxed and meditative state.

However, before we do this, it is a good idea to have a small check list of practical reminders. This will help avoid any unnecessary interruptions of the process of creative visualization.

1. *Possible distractions*: Be sure that the room you are in does not look onto a busy street – if it does, close the blinds or curtains to remove distractions. Have you remembered to unplug the phone or turn on the answering machine?
2. *Air*: How is the air and ventilation in your room? If you use machines or computers there daily, maybe you should consider acquiring an ionizer (if you do not have one already) to neutralize the ions. Also, you may have been burning incense – a lovely idea and something most children like. However, too much can interfere with the breathing exercises as it often causes a dry throat. Also be sure no-one has smoked in your room prior to your session!
3. *Light*: Is the light comfortable for closing your eyes (no glaring sunlight or 100 watt light bulbs?).
4. *Music*: If you have been using up-beat or fast music for the creative movement, be sure to counteract it with slow 'coming down' music as you begin the breathing process.

The sound of waves lapping on the shore can also be very helpful in creating a natural rhythm for the breathing to follow (see recommended music list).

5. *Seating*: If you are uncomfortable sitting on the floor, try using a large cushion. Failing that, you can sit in an upright chair. Wherever you choose to sit, it is essential that you both (or all) maintain a straight spine. This is to assist the flow of energy and your level of concentration.

Finally check the energy level of your child. At this stage, if children are tired they often want to lie down. This is not advisable as they may fall asleep during the process. If however your child is still not relaxed and centered you may wish to do the following exercise together.

Lie down on your back, placing support (such as a book or a small pillow) of about two inches in height under your head. Bend your knees until they point towards the ceiling and place the soles of your feet flat on the floor, hip-width apart. Let your hands rest on your hip bones, elbows resting on the floor. Now simply relax in this position for a few minutes, breathing deeply and evenly. Visualize your entire back sinking into the floor and feel all the tension running out of your body and into the ground. Take advantage of this moment and check that you yourself are in a state of calm, centered equilibrium. In my experience as both a teacher and parent, the state that I am in – whether I believe it is visible or not – profoundly affects the child or children and the processes involved in creative visualization. I have found it to be vital to a session that I myself am centered and in a state of complete calm and focus.

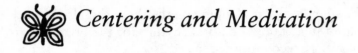 *Centering and Meditation*

You and your child are now ready to begin the process of centering and entering a meditative state of mind. For both this and the process of creative visualization to follow (Part 3), you may find it useful to pre-record your own voice reading the processes until – as with previous exercises – you are more familiar with the contents of these pages or you have developed your own visualizations.

The following are basic processes for centering and for entering into a meditative state that I have found to be most suited for children of all ages. All the processes progress naturally from the breathing exercises to create the relaxed and focused state of mind from which creative visualization will be most effective. As in previous chapters there are several different processes to choose from. You may find one that is more to the liking of your family than the others. Nevertheless it can be an advantage to change processes from time to time.

Be sure you have prepared your chosen process beforehand. Speak in a calm, soft but audible voice – somewhat slower than you normally do. Pause regularly so that all you say may be absorbed. Check regularly that your voice does not sound monotonous.

Process 1

Breathing deeply and evenly, focus on a point in front of you and slightly upwards. As you focus on this point, feel your eyelids getting heavier and heavier until they close. Do not resist – just let them close. Now bring your attention to your heart. You may want to place your hand on your heart. Feel the rhythm of your heartbeat. Is it slowing down or is it even? Keep all your attention on your heart. If other thoughts enter your head just let them float on by like petals on the river and bring your attention back to your heart. Holding your attention there, think of something or someone that you love – maybe a pet, a hug or your favorite place to be. Feel what that thought does to your heart. Does it make the area of your heart feel different? Hold that nice loving feeling in your heart for a little while, really hold onto it. Enjoy just how nice it feels. . . . *(be quiet for a few minutes or as long as your child's attention span is capable of. It is at this point that the creative visualization of your choice (see Part 3) is appropriate to introduce. When the creative visualization is complete, pause for a moment. If you have been playing relevant music in the background (see recommended music list), slowly turn down the volume until it is almost inaudible. As you resume speaking slightly speed up your voice. As you near the end of the process let your voice return to its normal pace and pitch.).* . . . Now gradually bring your attention back to your heart again. . . . Has your heartbeat changed at all? Feel the love inside your heart and send it all around your body. Feel the nice loving sensation everywhere. Now bring your attention to your breathing. Has that slowed down? Now very gradually bring your attention back into this room and when you are ready you can open your eyes.

Process 2

Breathe deeply and naturally and focus on a point in front of you, slightly upwards. Keep focusing on this point until your eyelids begin to feel heavy. . . . Feel them becoming heavier and heavier until they finally close. Feel how relaxed and heavy they are. Now listen to your own breathing, focusing on the rhythm. Be very still as you feel your breathing. Imagine you are a wave on the sea. . . . *(here it often helps to play a tape of gentle wave sounds, softly in the background).* . . . feel yourself washing up on the shore. . . . and out to sea again. . . . *(try to follow the rhythm of the waves. Your child's breathing rhythm will also follow!).* . . . in onto the shore and out to sea. . . . in and out. . . . in and out. . . . feel that you *are* the wave, that you *are* the sea. . . . (*be quiet for a few minutes or for as long as your child's attention span permits. At this point the creative visualization of your choice can be introduced. When you have completed the creative visualization, pause for a moment before you continue*). . . . See if you can feel a peacefulness inside you. . . . a deep, deep peacefulness. . . . that is deeper and quieter than you feel when you sleep. . . . be very still and *feel* the peace. . . . feel the silence. . . . enjoy the stillness and the peace for a moment. . . . (*be quiet for a minute or so and slowly turn down the volume of any music or sound effects you may have been using, until it is inaudible. Slightly speed up your voice as you continue this process, returning it to its normal speed and pitch by the end of the process.*). . . . Now slowly bring your attention back to your breathing. . . . Has it slowed down at all?. . . . How about your heartbeat?. . . . Feel your heartbeat for a moment. . . . Now gradually bring your attention back to this room and when you are ready you can open your eyes.

Process 3

Breathe easily and naturally and focus on a point in front of you and slightly upwards. Focus on this point until your eyelids begin to feel heavy. Now let them close, feeling how nice and relaxed your eyes feel. Now bring your attention to your heart – you may place your hand on your heart if you wish – and feel the rhythm of your heartbeat. Feel how nice and warm it feels around your heart. Now think of something that makes you feel love. . . . a kitten or a rabbit. . . . or a field full of pretty flowers. . . . a big hug from your favorite person. . . . feel how that makes your heart feel even warmer. Now feel your heart slowly getting bigger and bigger as it fills up with more love for all the animals and all the people in the whole world. Feel how much love you have for everyone. . . . and of course for yourself! Really enjoy that feeling for a moment. . . . Now feel yourself beginning to get smaller. . . . smaller and smaller and smaller until you are so small that you can fit inside your heart! Feel how nice it feels to be inside your heart. . . . how warm to be surrounded by all that love. . . . (*pause for a moment or for as long as your child's attention span holds. Then begin your chosen creative visualization process. When this is complete, be quiet for a moment. Gradually turn down the volume of any music you may have been playing until it is quite inaudible. As you begin to speak again, slightly speed up your voice.*). . . . Now be inside your heart again, surrounded by all that love . . . . Gradually feel yourself getting bigger, bigger and bigger until you are your normal size again. Now listen to your heartbeat. Is it different? You can bring your attention back into this room again and whenever you are ready you can open your eyes.

Process 4

Breathe deeply and evenly. Focus on a point in front of you and slightly upwards. As you focus on this point your eyelids will begin to feel heavy. Let them become heavier and heavier until they close, heavily and relaxed. Leave your attention with your breathing for a few moments. . . . now take your attention to your heart. . . . listen to your heartbeat, try to hear your heartbeat from within. . . . Now imagine above your head a beautiful fountain. This fountain is your own special fountain and it can look any way you want it to look. It can be any colour you want it to be . . . it can even have spots on it or stripes if you want! This fountain is filled with a beautiful white light, a white light that fills the fountain up until it overflows and pours out of the fountain just the way it should. See the beautiful white light pouring down from the fountain onto your head, onto the top of your head. Feel it splashing down on the crown of your head and pouring down across your face and down the back of your head and neck. Feel it gushing and splashing as it runs across your shoulders, chest and back and down onto your stomach and into your lap. Feel it streaming down your back and down both of your arms and both of your legs. Feel it pouring down you until it runs across your hands and feet and out past your fingers and toes into the earth. Feel yourself completely covered in and filled with this beautiful white light until you are part of it, part of the beautiful white light. Just enjoy how this feels for a moment. . . . (*be silent for a few minutes or until your child's attention begins to wander. Introduce your chosen creative visualization. When this is complete, gradually turn down any music or sound effects you may have been playing. Pause for a moment and as you speak again gradually speed up your voice a little.*). . . . Now bring your attention back to your heartbeat . . . can you feel it from within?. . . . Transfer your attention to your breathing . . . to the area around you . . . and to the room we are in. When you are ready you can open your eyes.

Process 5

Place a lit candle in the centre of the circle and ask your child or children to look at it, focusing all their attention on the flame. Encourage them to keep staring at the flame until they feel like closing their eyes. Let them close their eyes. Begin the process when everyone has closed their eyes. . . . Now see the reflection of the candle flame inside your head. See a flame just like the flame of the candle inside your head. Concentrate on the yellow of the flame for a moment . . . (*pause*) . . . now concentrate on the blue part of the flame . . . (*pause*) . . . now focus on the white of the flame . . . (*pause*) . . . Now feel the temperature of the flame. Feel yourself getting warmer and warmer, lighter and brighter. Feel yourself becoming part of the flame. . . . one with the warm bright light of the flame. Feel how warm and calm and centered you are. . . . now just *be* there for a moment. . . . (*be still for a few minutes or for as long as your child's attention span holds. Follow this by introducing the creative visualization of your choice. When this is complete, pause for a moment. If any music is playing in the background, slowly turn down the volume until it is no longer audible. As you begin to speak again, speed up your voice slightly*). . . . Now gradually bring your attention back to the feeling of warmth and to the point within you where you saw the flame. Focus on your own breathing. Now bringing your attention back to the room around you, take a deep breath and when you are ready you can open your eyes.

Process 6

Breathing deeply and evenly gently close your eyes, feeling all the muscles in your face relaxing. Bring your attention to the point between your eyebrows, inside your head. Keep breathing deeply and evenly, deeply and evenly. Imagine that behind that point, behind your eyes, there is a small door. Behind that door are some stairs leading down to your heart. We are now going to go down those stairs slowly and steadily. For each step you take you are going to become more and more relaxed as you go deeper and deeper inside yourself. There are ten steps to your heart and for each one you will be more relaxed. Here we go. . . . one. . . . two. . . . deeper. . . . three. . . . four. . . . more relaxed. . . . five. . . . six. . . . deeper still. . . . seven. . . . even more relaxed. . . . eight. . . . even deeper. . . . nine. . . . TEN. . . . you are now inside your heart, in a deep, relaxed and wonderful state of mind. Feel all the love there is in your heart. . . . now just stay there and enjoy this state for a while. . . . (*be quiet for a few minutes or however long your child's attention span lasts. Then introduce the creative visualization you have chosen. When this is complete, slowly turn down the volume of any music you have been playing. As you resume speaking, slightly speed up your voice and when you near the end of the process let your voice return to its normal speed and pitch*). . . . Now slowly bring your attention back to your heart. I will count backwards from ten to one and when I reach the number one you will be wide awake, you will feel great and you will open your eyes. Ten. . . . nine. . . . eight. . . . stretch a little. . . . seven. . . . waking up. . . . six. . . . five. . . . your eyes feel rested and refreshed. . . . four. . . . three. . . . feeling great. . . . two. . . . ONE! Open your eyes, you are wide awake, feeling great!

Process 7

Breathe deeply and naturally and focus on a point in front of you and slightly upwards. Keep your focus on this point until your eyelids begin to feel heavy. Let them close gently. Now bring your attention to your heart. It is as though you place your hand on your heart. Feel the rhythm of the heartbeat. Focus all your attention and awareness on your heart. Think of someone you love and feel the warmth in your heart area. Now take your awareness to your feet and toes and legs. Feel all the energy in these parts of your body. Now pull all this energy up and away from your toes, feet and legs and draw it into your heart. Now take your awareness to your head, to the crown of your head, your face and your neck. Feel all the energy there. Now draw all that energy down into your heart. Now take all your awareness out into both your shoulders, arms, hands and fingers. Feel all the energy there. Now draw all that energy into your heart. Now take your awareness to the area around your body. Feel the energy there. Now pull all the energy into your heart. Feel all that energy in your heart. Now feel the love in your heart. Feel your heart swelling up with all that loving energy. Now send that loving energy to someone who needs it. . . . and then to yourself. Keep feeling it, sending it and enjoying it for a while. . . . (*pause for a few minutes or for as long as your child's attention span is capable of. Begin your chosen creative visualization. When it is completed, be still for a moment. Slowly turn down the volume of any background music you may have been playing until it is inaudible. As you begin to speak again, slightly speed up your voice until, at the end of the process, your voice is normal in speed and pitch.*). . . . Now gradually bring your attention back in to your heart. Feel all the love inside and know that it is always there. Now bring your attention to your breathing . . . . and then back into this room. Take a deep breath and whenever you are ready, open your eyes!

For a list of appropriate music and sound effects for these meditations and the following creative visualizations, please check the recommended music list at the back of this book. Music should be played at a relatively low volume so as not to distract from your voice. Be sure that your tape is long enough for your purpose. If you or your child find music a distraction, refrain from using it.

PART THREE

Creative Visualizations

The creative visualizations in this book are meant to be integrated with the meditations and used within the structured context outlined. That being said, there are many ways to implement them and you will undoubtedly discover and develop your own personal way in time.

When guiding a creative visualization with children it is essential that all the preparatory work has been done (that is, release of tension, focus of the energy and relaxation into a meditative state). As you progress, the time you need to spend on each process will lessen, although you may *wish* to spend longer on certain processes that you particularly enjoy! Meanwhile, do take all the time needed to help your child into the right state of mind so that he or she may really benefit, from day one!

As in the meditations, keep your voice soft but audible and speak slowly, with frequent pauses. You do not need to follow the script word for word – improvise over it, use your own imagination and apply your knowledge of your child's individual needs.

Each of the following visualizations can be used for all ages, although I suggest that you adapt the language to suit the age and mentality of your child if necessary.

If you use any sound effects or music remember, it is there to help concentrate the energy, add to the atmosphere and *support* the process.

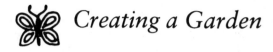 *Creating a Garden*

Each one of these visualizations follows on naturally from a meditation and is completed by the 'coming out' process of the same meditation (see previous chapter of meditations).

THE PATH

I want you to see before you a path in nature – any way you want it to be – wide, narrow, winding, straight, by a stream or by the sea, in a meadow or a forest – whatever you like. . . . Now I want you to walk down your path until you come to a tree, a tree with many, many branches. This is the Trouble Tree, the tree where you hang all your troubles. Pause a moment and offload all your troubles – no matter how small. Hang them all on the tree before you move on. . . . Be sure you haven't forgotten any!. . . . Now continue on down your path. If there are any rocks or twigs or other obstacles, stop and gently move them to the side. Give them some of all that love you have in your heart and move on. Soon you arrive at a small gate covered in your favorite flowers. Smell their lovely fragrance as you gently push open the gate. As you step through your gate you enter into the most beautiful garden you have ever seen. It is exactly the way you want it to be and it is all your very own. . . .: All the colors in your garden are very bright and beautiful. The sun is shining brightly and the birds are singing a welcoming song. You feel so safe and peaceful. . . . Wander through your garden for a while and explore it. . . . (*Pause for a few minutes or for as long as your child's attention span holds.*). . . . Now before you leave I want you to thank your garden for being there for you and for being so perfect!

Know that your garden will *always* be there for you whenever you need it. . . . (*Return to the appropriate section of the meditation process*).

This is a basic visualization that I have found to be very effective both as a frame and as a foundation for further or more specific visualizations. You can build on it – which I do in many of the visualizations to follow – or you can just use it as it is. Alone it is especially helpful when a child is ill, worrying about something in particular or needs help to feel secure.

In addition to your sessions, you *can* use this visualization in isolation, much as you would use storytelling. In my experience it can be helpful when a child has difficulty falling asleep or when there is a challenge to overcome such as a hospital stay.

THE PROFESSOR TREE

See before you your path in nature. Wander down it until you come to your Trouble Tree. Stop by your Trouble Tree and hang up any troubles you might have today. Remember, it doesn't matter *what* they are. . . . the Trouble Tree has so many, many branches, there is room for any and all kinds of troubles. . . . Now move on until you come to your gate. Stop and smell the beautiful flowers growing on your gate. As you open your gate you notice that the sun seems to shine even more brightly. Inside your garden the sky above you is the brightest blue you have ever seen. Around you birds are chirping and the grass beneath your feet is soft and cool. You walk through your garden until you come to a very large redwood tree. It is so tall that it reaches up way past the clouds. . . . you cannot see the top of it! The trunk of the tree is huge and at the base of it is a small opening – just big enough for you to fit through. As you look closely at the tree trunk it appears to have a face – a very kind and wise face, like a kindly professor. It seems to be beckoning to you and you very gently step through the opening and into the trunk. As your eyes get accustomed to the light you see that the centre of the trunk is hollow and on the inside are lots of tiny doors. Each door leads to a part of the bark and within the bark is all the wisdom you will ever need. Do you have a question to ask? Any question that you need an answer to, will do. . . . As you think of your question, the tiny door to the part of the bark that has your answer opens, as if by magic. Go towards the open door now and receive your answer. . . . It may be there in writing . . . or as a picture. . . . or you may hear it. . . . Now step out of the tree trunk and into your garden. Turn to thank your Professor Tree for being there. He is telling you that he will *always* be there, whenever you need an answer. As you wander towards your garden gate, thank your garden for being there and know that it will always be there, no matter when you need it. . . . (*Return to the appropriate section of the meditation process*).

If your child sometimes does not get an answer in the Professor Tree, assure him or her that it will come soon enough. Maybe there wasn't room in the tiny door for the answer or maybe it just wasn't ready? My experience is that they almost always get an answer. However, sometimes it is personal or private. Do not probe your child for their question or their answer. If they want you to know they will share it with you in good time.

CLOUDS OF PERCEPTION

See before you your path in nature. Now walk along it until you come to your Trouble Tree. Pause and hang up any troubles you might have today. Remember your Trouble Tree takes all kinds of troubles!. . . . Now walk along your path until you arrive at your gate. The flowers growing on your gate are covered in dew drops today. Don't they smell lovely? Open your gate now and go into your garden. As you wander through the grass you notice a gentle breeze caressing your skin and mingling with the warmth of the sun. The grass is soft and dry so you decide to lie down for a while. As you look up towards the sky you see a few small fluffy white clouds floating by. You watch them and discover that their shapes create different images. In one cloud you can see the figure of a

lady. . . . as you keep watching the image changes to one of an
elf. . . . soon it changes to an old man. . . . then a rabbit. . . .
stay and watch the clouds for a little while and see how many
different shapes and images they make as you look at them in
different ways. . . . Now it is time for you to leave your garden.
As you say goodbye to the clouds you thank the garden for
being there and know that it will always be there for you
whenever you need it. . . . (*Return to the appropriate section
of the meditation process.*)

LAKE OF REFLECTION

I want you to go to your path in nature and wander down
it. . . . until you come to your Trouble Tree. If you have any
troubles today, hang them up on the tree before you move on.
. . . Now keep going along your path until you arrive at your
gate. There are a couple of beautiful butterflies fluttering
around the flowers on your gate. Watch them alight on the
flowers, enjoying the ride as you swing open the gate. Today
your garden is filled with the scent of fruit blossoms and the
birds are singing happily. You go for a walk in your garden,
passing the tall Professor Tree. . . . do you want to stop and
ask a question?. . . . You continue through your garden, past
some other trees, down a slope, across the grass. . . . until you
come to a small lake, a beautiful blue-green lake. The sun is
shining above it, casting a bright white light that reflects off
the water making it look as if a thousand diamonds are dancing
on the lake's surface. You pause and become aware of every
movement on the lake. . . . every ripple on the water's surface.
. . . the air is very still and the lake is calm. . . . peaceful. . . . as
you look a small raft comes floating towards you. . . . you climb
onto it, knowing that everything in your garden is completely
safe. Slowly the raft takes you out into the center of the lake,
gliding across the water like a graceful swan. You lie on the
raft looking over the edge and into the water. It is as clear as
glass and you can see yourself just as if you were looking into
a mirror. . . . what else do you see?. . . . The raft is gently gliding
back to the edge of the lake now. . . . Slowly you step out onto

the grassy bank and wave goodbye to the raft. You wander back through your garden knowing that you can come there any time you want. Thank your garden as you leave. . . . (*Return to the appropriate section of the meditation process.*)

CRYSTAL MOUNTAIN

I want you to see before you your path in nature. Walk down it until you arrive at your Trouble Tree. Do you have any troubles to hang up today?. . . . Now move on until you come to your gate. Smell the sweet scent of the fresh flowers as you open your gate. As you enter your garden today you notice a small pathway of pebbles to one side. . . . and you decide to follow it. It twists and winds its way through your garden, past a multitude of beautiful flowers, bushes and plants. . . . Soon you arrive at the corner of a hedge. As you turn the corner you see before you a magnificent mountain. It is multi-colored and looks like a giant crystal. As you move closer you see that it has many naturally inbuilt steps. . . . you decide to climb them! As you step onto the first step you notice that the color all along the base of the mountain is red. A bright fiery red. You notice that there are bright red flowers growing on one side and a cherry tree weighed down with bright red cherries on the other. The red flowers are giving off the most exotic scent and you decide to pick a cherry. As you bite into it the sweet juice fills your mouth. . . . mmmmmmmmmmmm. . . . You move on a few steps up the Crystal Mountain and you become aware of the now brilliant orange color under your feet. . . . You seem to be in an orange grove for there are succulent oranges weighing down the trees all around you. Maybe you'd like to have some orange juice. . . . straight out of an orange. . . . Now you take a few steps further up the mountain and you find that this level is a strong, bright yellow. There are yellow flowers everywhere. . . . tall ones, short ones, big ones and little ones. . . . There is a small stream to one side and you decide to sit in it to refresh yourself. . . . a lemon tree shades you as you bathe and the strong fresh scent of lemons refreshes you even more. . . . A few more steps up the mountain is a wonderful lush green. It is just like being in the rainforest. There are so many beautiful birds flying in and out of the hundreds of trees and all your favorite animals are there to greet you. . . . Now move up to the next level and everywhere around you is blue. You have never seen such a beautiful blue. . . . To one side of the mountain you notice the sea and dolphins playing in the clear blue water. You dive into the blue sea and swim and play with the dolphins for a while. . . . As you come back to the mountain you step up above the blue rock and all at once everything around you is violet. . . . it's like being on a giant amethyst. . . . the light reflects off the rocks and everything around you sparkles!. . . . As you finally step up onto the top of your mountain, all around you becomes white. . . . brilliant white. All your favorite thoughts and dreams live here. Your favorite things and beings are here . . . angels, fairies, clouds and sunbeams . . . whatever you want to be here is here. . . . all bathed in a brilliant white light. . . . I will leave you now for a little while to enjoy your Crystal Mountain. Maybe you want to explore a little?. . . . (*pause*). . . . As you leave your crystal mountain you thank it for being there. . . . and you know that you can come back anytime you want. Thank your garden as well. . . . for always being there for you. . . . (*Return to the appropriate section of the meditation process*).

It may be an advantage, ahead of this visualization, to familiarize your child with crystals if you have not done so already.

THE MAGIC CARPET

See before you your path in nature. Take a leisurely walk down your path until you get to your Trouble Tree. Pause to see if you have any troubles to hang on this tree today. If you do, go ahead and hang them there. Be sure not to forget any!. . . . Now continue down your path until you come to your garden gate. Pause to enjoy the beautiful flowers growing on your gate. Enjoy their perfume. Now open your gate and go into your garden. As you wander through your garden you feel the sun warming you. The birds and insects sound like a choir today. The grass looks greener than ever! Feeling its softness beneath your feet you look down. . . . a little ahead of you there appears to be something patterned lying in the grass. . . . You run forward to see what it is. . . . There before you is a brightly colored carpet, lying in the middle of the grass. You bend down and touch it. . . . it has a nice soft velvety feel. . . . slowly you step onto it and sit down. It feels really comfortable. . . . it feels almost like sitting on air. . . . gradually you realize that you *are* sitting on air, for your carpet has risen and is hovering a few inches above the ground. How exciting! Let us see if it can really fly!. . . . It is indeed a magic carpet. . . . it is rising higher and higher, up, up, up, up you go. . . . past the tree tops, up through and beyond the clouds. . . . up, up, up in the air, away from the Earth until our planet is just a small ball beneath you. Higher and higher you go, up into the atmosphere until you are flying between the stars. As you sit on your magic carpet up there amongst the stars, you gaze down upon Mother Earth and send her all the love you can. Isn't it great to be able to do this?. . . . Now you may want to spend some some time flying around the stars and enjoying yourself. . . . (*pause for as long as your child's attention span permits*). . . . Now your magic carpet is beginning to descend. . . . wave goodbye to the stars as you fly down, down, down, down. . . . planet Earth looks bigger and bigger as you come nearer and nearer. . . . through the clouds, down past the tree tops. . . . and very gently your magic carpet lands on the soft grass in your garden. As you leave the magic carpet and your garden, thank them both for being there for you. . . . (*Return to the appropriate section of the meditation process.*)

THE RAINBOW BRIDGE

I want you to see before you your path in nature. Wander down it until you come to your Trouble Tree. Now hang all your troubles on this tree before you continue down your path. . . . Now as you walk down your path towards your gate, remember to remove any obstacles you may come across, gently and with love. Upon reaching your garden gate notice all the different colors of the flowers growing there. Smell their sweet scent as you gently push open the gate. Leisurely wander through your garden, enjoying all the different sights, sounds and smells. . . . stroke your favorite flower and feel the softness of the petals. . . . Notice that it has just finished raining in your garden. The sun is shining now and small drops of rain water are shimmering on the leaves of the trees. The grass is moist and the air is fresh. As you look across your garden you see several rainbows. . . . They look as if they are building bridges between the trees. There are so many of them, it makes you want to jump for joy! Way beyond all these smaller rainbows is one gigantic one! You begin to walk towards it. You know that in your garden magic things can happen and you may actually *reach* the rainbow if you just keep going!. . . . On and on you go, moving swiftly now, through your garden, towards the giant rainbow. Nearer and nearer until. . . . as if by magic, you are standing right underneath the rainbow! It is like a great big enormous bridge, reaching from one side of your garden to the other. You decide to venture over it. You walk across to one side and begin to climb. As you look down, you realize that you yourself have become *all* the colors of the rainbow. . . . red, orange, yellow, green, blue, indigo and violet. In being on the rainbow you have become part of it. . . . As you near the top of the Rainbow Bridge you see a figure coming towards you from the other side of the bridge. . . . it is a rainbow friend! . . . I will leave you now for a little while to play on the rainbow with your rainbow friend. . . . (*pause*). . . . Now it is time to leave the rainbow and your rainbow friend. Thank them both for being there. . . . then thank your garden as you leave. You know that they are all there for you any time you need them. . . . (*Return to the appropriate section of the meditation process.*)

THE HEALING FAIRIES

See before you your path in nature. You walk along it and pass your Trouble Tree. See if you have any troubles to hang up today. Then continue along your path until you come to your garden gate. What a beautiful gate it is today. . . . covered in the most colorful and sweet smelling of flowers you can possibly imagine. This must be the most special gate ever! You gently push it open, pass through it and pause to admire your special gate again as it closes behind you. Walking away from the gate and into your garden, you notice a rustling sound behind you. You turn around. . . . and see several tiny heart-shaped faces peering out from between the flowers on your gate. As you look closer you see that the faces belong to little fairies gradually emerging from behind the flowers and leaves. First one fairy emerges. . . . then another. . . . and then another until about ten fairies are fluttering their wings in front of you. They are all carrying little feather dusters and have warm, welcoming smiles on their faces. They begin to sing;

> Let us show you what we can do
> To help you if you're feeling blue.

Then they take your hands and lead you through your garden. . . . (*pause*). . . . You arrive at a small secluded beach. The sand is soft, dry and warm. Here the fairies ask you to make yourself comfortable. They busy themselves around you with their dusters. You feel relaxed and peaceful and you can feel the love of the fairies in your own heart. . . . The fairies sing:

> Wherever it is that you're not full of zeal
> We'll bring in our dusters and help you to heal.

I am sure there is somewhere you would like to feel better. . . . Maybe you would just like to enjoy being pampered by the Healing Fairies. . . . (*pause for as long as your child's attention span permits*). . . . As you thank the fairies and leave them behind, you know that they will always be there if you need them. . . . just like your garden is. . . . (*Return to the appropriate section of the meditation process.*)

This last garden visualization can be used effectively when your child is not feeling well or is suffering from the normal aches and pains that go with growing up! I have also found it to be both useful and effective to use separately, when a child is going to see a doctor or dentist. It helps the child relax, handle the situation with more calm and can often help ease any temporary pain the child might be experiencing. In my personal experience it has also helped speed the healing process when a child is ill.

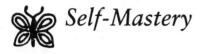 *Self-Mastery*

Each one of these visualizations follows on naturally from a meditation and is completed by the 'coming out' process of the same meditation (see chapter Centering and Meditation). However, the visualizations in this chapter can also be used in isolation, to help combat fears and build self-confidence in the physical situation and at the actual time it is required.

NIGHTMARES

If your child suffers from frequent nightmares, is frightened by 'monsters under the bed' or sees 'monsters' and other scary beings at night, do the following visualization within a meditation, once. If or when the nightmares recur, do the visualization again *immediately or as soon as possible*, preferably as soon as your child is in sufficient control of him or herself to follow the process. If your child is old enough to remember the visualization and do it alone, encourage them and remind them of it just before bedtime.

Know that you are now in a safe place – it is quiet and peaceful and there is love all around you, and filling up your heart. You are safe and at peace. Now I want you to turn around and look at the monster, facing it. It is quite safe because now *you* are in charge! Now stretch both arms forward, towards the monster. Stretch out all your fingers. As you stretch, see the monster getting smaller and smaller. Keep stretching. The monster is shrinking more and more as you stretch, getting smaller and smaller until it is small enough to fit on the palm of your hand. It is still shrinking, getting smaller until it is just the size of a pin head. Now you can befriend it. . . . play with it. . . . do whatever you like with it. . . . bounce it around like a ball if you want. . . . play with it any way you want! (*If your child wishes to throw it out of the window or anywhere else, let them do what feels natural to them.*)

ACHES AND PAINS FROM TENSION

If your child suffers from aches and pains due to tension, such as headaches, tummy aches, or the like, the following visualization can be of great help. Do the visualization once, within a meditation. Following this, have your child perform the action from the visualization (in this case, drinking a glass of water) while re-affirming the affirmation process from the visualization. If the aches and pains persist, take your child to a medical practitioner to ascertain whether they are due to something other than tension.

I want you to see before you a large glass. Now see this glass filling up with drinking water until it is full. Know that in this water there are a million invisible magic crystals that are going to take away your ——ache. Now take a deep breath and then let all the air out again. Now see yourself placing the glass of water to your lips and drinking the water. As the water runs down your throat and into your stomach, feel your ——ache running down and out of your body as the magic crystals in the water wash it away. Know that as soon as you have finished drinking the water, your ——ache will be completely gone! (*brief pause*) Your ——ache is now gone and you are feeling much better than before!

In my experience, this visualization has helped with temper tantrums as well as aches and pains. However, this has been in cases where the child recognizes that the tantrums are not doing them any good and he or she *wishes* to control or eliminate them. No matter what the problem, if it is tension-related this visualization can be of value.

ANGER

If your child is prone to anger and frequent temper tantrums, do the following visualization once within a meditation process (if the problem is serious, you may want to do it two or three times this way). Then encourage your child to use the visualization themselves whenever you sense anger brewing in them. After some time, the visualization prior to this one can also be used.

See yourself in a bare room. See yourself being angry – see how your face looks and how your body feels. . . . Now leave that behind. . . . See instead before you your garden. See yourself now in your garden, cuddling your very favorite pet, animal or soft toy. See how happy you are. See how your face looks and how your body feels. . . . Now say to yourself that next time you feel yourself becoming angry, stop and go to your garden to cuddle your favorite pet for a moment. When you have done that, look at what was making you angry again. See it from where you are in your garden, not from your anger. *Know* that you will feel much better for doing this. Your face, your body, your feelings and *all* of you will feel much better!

IRRATIONAL FEARS

If your child is prone to nervousness and suffers from irrational fears, all the garden visualizations can be very helpful. However, do be sure that the fears *are* irrational and that there is nothing practical or physical that can be done about them.

An ideal time to do the garden visualizations is at bedtime. The more frequently you do them, the better. The following visualizations can be used for specific fears.

Know now that you are in a very safe place. Now I want you to turn around and look at what you are afraid of. Look at your fear of. . . . (*name whatever it is*). I want you to make the fear into a cloud. . . . what color is it? Now I want you to point at the cloud. As you point at the cloud, see it begin to shrink. It is getting smaller and smaller. Put your other hand out and catch it as it becomes small enough to fit on your hand. Look at it. It is just a little cloud and a cloud is made of water. Close your hand now and feel the cloud evaporate. Open your hand and see only a few little drops of water. Hold your hand out until it dries. . . . There, now your cloud has gone, your fear has evaporated, disappeared! (*You may have to do this a few times before it takes hold, depending on the extent and intensity of the fear.*)

WORRIES AND CONCERNS

If your child exhibits worry and concern beyond what is normal for your child's age, the following visualization can be helpful. Do it within a meditation once or twice. Then encourage your child to use the visualization him or herself whenever the feeling of anxiousness appears.

See yourself in a wide open space. See yourself being worried. See how your face looks and how it feels. See how your shoulders and neck and hands look and feel. . . . Now leave that behind. . . . see instead before you your special garden. See yourself now in your garden, doing your very favorite thing, really enjoying yourself!. . . . (*pause long enough for your child to really get in touch with the enjoyment of doing their favorite thing*). . . . See how happy you are. See how your face looks and how it feels. See how relaxed your shoulders, neck and hands are. . . . Now tell yourself that whenever you feel yourself becoming worried or concerned, stop! Then go to your special garden and enjoy doing your very favorite thing. When you have done that, look again at what made you worry. See it from the comfort and joy of your garden. Is it worth worrying so much about?. . . . Know that doing this process will always make you feel safe and secure inside yourself.

For the above visualization and the visualization for anger, it is a prerequisite that your child has already created their own garden (see chapter Creating a Garden) and is familiar with the various garden visualizations.

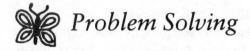 *Problem Solving*

Using creative visualization for problem solving with children often involves two stages. The first one – the one that will always be used – is helping them to tap into their own inner knowing. The second one is helping them to manifest any changes that problem solving may require. I have divided each visualization into two parts. Depending on the problem, part two will not always be needed.

Varying images are used for different age groups, as older children often prefer abstract images when problem solving and younger children relate better to more concrete images. That being said, please use the guidelines for age loosely – your child's individuality may dictate a very different choice. It is OK if your adolescent prefers the visualization for pre-schoolers and if your seven year old would rather use the one for teenagers!

Each one of the visualizations follows on naturally from a meditation and is completed by the 'coming out' process of the same meditation (see chapter on Centering and Meditation).

THE PROFESSOR TREE

Pre-school to pre-adolescent. A prerequisite for this visualization is the creation of your child's own special garden – see chapter on Creating a Garden.

See before you the gate to your own special garden. See what beautiful flowers it is covered in today. Smell their scent as you push open your gate. . . . Now walk through it and into your garden. Wander through your garden until you come to your

Professor Tree – that tall, tall redwood tree with the very, very large trunk! Walk up to the opening in the trunk and gently, very gently step through the opening and into the trunk. As your eyes become accustomed to the gloom you see how very large and hollow the inside of the trunk is. All around you are lots of little doors on the inside of the trunk, each one leading to a section of the bark. Within the bark of this great tree lies all the wisdom you will ever need. On the front of each little door is marked a word. One says 'Family', another 'School' and another '————' (*fill in the subject matter referring to your child's problem, if you know it*). Now take out your question/problem and go up to the door where it belongs. Gently open the door and place your question/problem inside. Now gently close the door again. As you wait for an answer, take a deep breath and inhale the wonderful scent of the tree. Take in with it some of all the energy within the tree and feel how nice it feels. Isn't it great to have your own special garden and tree where you can come any time you want? Think of all the nice things you do in your garden and see if those thoughts don't make your heart feel good and loving. Enjoy that feeling for a moment. . . . (*pause briefly*). . . . As you enjoy your nice feeling, the little door with your answer opens, all by itself. Go up to it and receive your answer in whatever form it takes. . . . (*pause*). . . . Now thank your tree for its wisdom and for being there for you. Step out of the trunk and walk through your garden. Thank your garden also for being there for you. . . . (*Return to the appropriate section of the meditation process or proceed with the second part of this visualization – whichever is relevant.*)

Just before you arrive at your gate, you notice a small field to the right. In the center of the field is a small platform. As you move closer you see that it is a stage, built with logs. In front of the stage are several rows of large toadstools. You decide to sit down on one and make yourself comfortable. You wonder whether anything will happen when you see a figure appear on the stage. It is you! The figure is you before you received the answer/solution (*delete as appropriate*) to your question/problem. What did you look like and how did you feel? What is the difference between the you watching on the toadstool and the you on the stage?. . . . What changes do you have to make now that you know the answer/solution?. . . . Watch yourself on the stage, making that change. . . . (*pause for a few minutes or until you sense that your child has completed the process or is becoming restless*). Now watch yourself bowing, having completed the change. Applaud yourself. . . . clapping enthusiastically you stand up and turn to leave. Thank the stage and the field in your garden for this experience!. . . . (*Return to the appropriate section in the meditation process.*)

THE PALACE

Primary school age to pre-adolescence.

See before you a beautiful scene in nature – whatever you like. A beach, rolling hills, a forest or a landscaped garden or any other scene in nature. Now I want you to walk through your scene, exploring it for a moment. . . . (*pause*). . . . You come upon a pathway in your scene and begin to walk along it. In the distance you see that the pathway ends in front of a large building. As you come closer, you see that the building is very beautiful. . . . it looks like a palace! Slowly you approach the palace, admiring its great majestic beauty. . . . There are two great golden doors at the center of the palace. The doors open as you walk towards them. Slowly you enter the palace. There are many rooms in this palace – in fact there are hundreds of rooms in this palace! On the door to each room is a sign. One says 'School', another says 'Friends' and third says 'Family' and yet another says '————————————' (*fill in the subject matter of your child's problem if you know it*). Behind each door is a room with a royal person or family in it. They have all the wisdom needed to solve any problem relating to the sign on their door! Now I want you to take out your question/problem (*delete as appropriate*) and go to the door that you need. Gently open it and go inside. . . . What do you see?. . . . Now present your question or problem to the royalty there and sit down on a cushion or in a chair to await their response. As you wait, notice the feel of the material you are sitting on. Is it velvet or silk or another material? How does it feel? A wonderful rich scent is in the air around you. Everything in the room is warm and beautiful. Feel yourself taking in all the warm and wonderful energies. Feel the area around your heart. . . . what is it in the room that makes you feel warm within your heart? . . . (*pause*). . . . As you enjoy your nice feelings, the royalty comes towards you with your answer/solution. Gracefully receive it, in whatever form it takes. . . . (*pause*). . . . Now thank your royalty for their wisdom and gracefully leave the room. Thank your palace as you leave it, for being there for you. (*Return to the appropriate section of the meditation process or proceed with the second part of this visualization, whichever is relevant.*)

As you walk through the large golden doors, a voice from just inside them calls you back. You return through the doors and go through another door where the voice that is calling you is coming from. Inside is a very comfortable looking classroom. It is furnished just the way you believe a classroom should be furnished. At one end is a large blackboard and a table with every conceivable colored chalk on it that you can imagine. The voice is coming from a window – you go to the window and look outside. There you see. . . . yourself. . . . as you were before you got your answer/solution, before you came into the palace. How did you feel then?. . . . How do you feel now?. . . . Do you have to make any changes now that you know the answer/solution?. . . . (*pause*). . . . Go to the blackboard and pick up your favorite colored chalk. . . . Now write down the change(s) you have to make on the blackboard. . . . See the words taking shape. . . . Repeat all you write in another color. . . . Fill the blackboard with the change(s) you are making. . . . Now step back and look at the blackboard. . . . Know that you have already made the change(s). . . . Give yourself the best grade you can get for such wonderful work! Write the grade at the top of the blackboard. . . . Thank the classroom for being there and for helping you to have this experience. . . . As you leave the palace and your beautiful place in nature, thank them both. . . . (*Return to the appropriate section of the meditation process.*)

THE HEART

Adolescents

Focus all your attention on your heart, thinking about something or someone you love. . . . Enjoy the good feeling this gives you. . . . Now take a deep breath and feel the feeling of warmth and love spreading through your body. . . . take another deep breath and feel it filling your whole body. . . . Now when you take another deep breath, feel the love filling up the area around your body. Feel the loving feeling spread to fill the room you are in. . . . Now take another breath and spread the feeling of love until it fills the building you are in. . . . breathe deeply and fill the street and area around the building. . . . Now fill the whole town with that feeling of love. . . . Take another deep breath and spread the feeling throughout your entire country. . . . Now take another deep breath and fill up the continent with the feeling of love. . . . Now the seas around the continent. . . . another deep breath and from the center of your heart feel the love reaching out and spreading across all the continents until it has covered the whole world. . . . Now take a deep breath and feel the love fill the atmosphere around the world. . . . Fill the universe with your love!. . . . (*pause*). . . . Keep focusing your attention on your heart. . . . Now feel yourself begin to grow smaller. . . . smaller and smaller and smaller until you are small enough to fit inside your heart. Take your question/problem (*delete as appropriate*) and place it there, knowing that the answer/solution you are seeking is right there, within your own heart. Feel just how nice it feels to have so much love in your heart, and know that all the wisdom you will ever need is there for you. . . . (*pause*). . . . Receive and accept your answer, however it comes to you. . . . Now *appreciate yourself* and your ability to feel so much love. Sincerely thank your heart and yourself for giving you this experience. . . . Now begin to feel yourself grow bigger, expanding and growing. . . . bigger and bigger until you are back to your normal size. (*Return to the appropriate section of the meditation process or proceed with the second part of this visualization, whichever is relevant.*)

Now imagine before you a large movie screen. Seat yourself in the center of the auditorium, right in front of the screen. A film begins. It is a film of you, before you received your answer/solution to your question/problem. What do you look like? How are you behaving? How do you feel?. . . . Do you need to make any changes, now that you have your answer/solution?. . . . The film stops and a new film begins. It is a film of you making the change(s) you have decided to make. . . . As the film progresses you see yourself after the change(s). . . . What do you look like now? How are you behaving? Do you feel any different?. . . . Now see yourself in front of the screen, receiving an award! The award is for having achieved such a positive change with such ease. Accept the award graciously. . . . a resounding applause greets you from the auditorium. Applaud yourself with enthusiasm. Thank yourself, the film, the screen and the auditorium!. . . . (*Return to the appropriate section of the meditation process*).

If your child occasionally does not receive an answer or solution to his or her question or problem, it is essential that they do not feel inadequate. To this end you must let them know that *no-one* will *always* receive an answer to their question immediately upon request. Let your child know that you also have experienced this and that sometimes the answers we seek come in a different way and at another time. Be sure that your child understands that when we are ready to receive an answer, the answer *will* come, in some form!

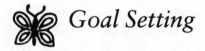 *Goal Setting*

Setting goals in life is surely a prerequisite for attaining them, whatever your age! However, the younger you are when you learn and understand this, the simpler it will be to remain focused on what you want throughout the more tumultuous adolescent and adult years. Equally, the *clearer* the goal, the more likely it will be to manifest.

The creative visualizations in this chapter are for clarifying, setting and focusing on a goal.

To clarify a goal, particularly for younger children, a preliminary talk may be necessary. Regardless of age, give your child the time and effort needed to insure that he or she is first completely clear about what he or she wants (their goal) and second, aware of the consequences of achieving it.

To stay focused on the goal, it is often necessary to repeat the visualization daily for a limited time period (the length of which will depend somewhat on the level of attainability of the goal).

A greater emphasis is placed on older children in these visualizations (that is, age ten upwards), although they can be used for younger children as well. As I have stated previously, your child's individuality must be your primary guideline.

Each visualization follows on naturally from a meditation and is completed by the 'coming out' process of the same meditation (see chapter on Centering and Meditation).

YOUR OFFICE

Focus all your attention on your heart, thinking about someone or something you love. . . . enjoy the feeling of warmth around your heart. . . . feel it spreading throughout your body. . . . just enjoy it for a moment. . . . (*pause*). . . . Now see before you a beautiful scene in nature. . . . any scene you like. . . . by the sea, in a forest, or you may even want it to be on another planet. . . . notice the colours in your scene. . . . now notice any scents. . . . notice the temperature. . . . is it hot or cold or just right?. . . . now notice any sounds you hear. . . . feel the peace in your scene. . . . feel the peace around you and within you. . . . now wander around a little and make yourself at home. . . . now that you feel completely at ease in your scene, you notice on a small hill quite near you, a small building. Go towards it. . . . you approach a door at the front of the building. . . . open it and enter the building. It is *your* building. Inside it you find an office. . . . your very own, special office, furnished exactly the way you want it to be. Notice the details in your office. . . . spend a little time exploring this room. . . .

Now sit down by the desk or table in your office. There is a pen and some paper there. I want you to write down now, the goal that you have decided to pursue. Write it down in detail, taking your time and doing it thoroughly. See the words forming on the paper as you write. . . . (*pause*). . . . Now I want you to call on your guide or special teacher. . . . This can be anyone you want it to be. . . . and this guide or teacher is going to come into your office through a door facing you. Look at the door now as it opens and your guide stands before you. . . . (*pause*). . . . You are going to ask your guide to show you what you have to do to achieve your goal. . . . Ask your guide now. . . . and just be with your guide, listening to all your guide has to tell you. . . . (*pause*). . . . Now turn towards a wall in your office that is covered by a screen. Watch the screen as a film is projected onto it. The film shows you achieving your goal. . . . How does it feel?. . . . Know now that you can reach your goal and that all you need is inside of you. . . . Thank your guide and your office for being there and know that they will always be there to help you with your goals. Leave your building now, closing the door behind you. . . . (*Return to the appropriate section of the meditation process*).

YOUR THEATER

Focus all your attention on your heart and think of something you love. . . . enjoy how that makes you feel. . . . Now see before you a large theater building. It is situated in the most perfect place and is designed exactly the way you like. . . . Now go into the theater through the front entrance or the stage door, whichever you prefer. . . . This is *your* theater. Wander through it for a while, exploring it. . . . Notice any particular color. . . . any special sounds. . . . any smells. . . . What is the temperature like?. . . . Feel the peace and quiet of your theater. . . . Now go into the auditorium and sit down on one of the seats near the center. . . . Feel the texture of the material on the seat. . . . Make yourself comfortable. . . . On the seat next to you is a glossy brochure. You pick it up and look at it. The brochure describes your goal. . . . very accurately and in full-page color photos! There are many photos in the brochure, each one equally descriptive of your goal. Take some time to look at each photo. Notice all the details and enjoy your brochure. . . . (*pause*). . . . You hear a noise now and look up. A director is walking onto the stage from the wings. It is your very own director and can therefore be whoever you want. . . . Your director begins to speak. . . . telling you about practice/rehearsals. . . . explaining what needs to be done before your goal can be achieved. . . . Listen to your director. . . . (pause). . . . Now your director leaves the stage and the lights dim. One large spotlight hits center stage. . . . and in it is you!. . . . Your play begins. It is the attainment of your goal being performed before your very eyes. . . . watch and enjoy it. . . . (pause). . . . Your play is complete and the curtain closes. You thank your director and the entire cast of players. You thank your theater and know that they will all be there for you whenever you need them. You leave your theater now, knowing that you *can* achieve the goal you have set yourself. . . . (*Return to the appropriate section of the meditation process*).

You can enhance the effect of these visualizations by suggesting that your child imagine the attainment of his or her goal – rekindling the *feeling* they had when 'seeing' it in their visualization – whenever performing any task or step towards their goal.

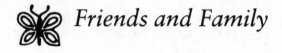

Friends and Family

Relationships with family and friends can be a challenge for every child and different approaches are needed at different times. Creative visualization can be used to help your child in the improvement of his or her relationships in most situations as it is effective on many levels. Visualization can assist the relationship even if only one of the parties uses it. Should two or more people be using it to improve the same situation or relationship, it can be just as effective whether they do it together or separately, simultaneously or at different times.

Whatever the relationship, the visualizations in this chapter can be used to help with conflict resolution, interrelating and as a precursor to effective listening (see chapter on Sharing). They can also be helpful when used prior to a session for conflict resolution, a discussion or any other communication aimed at settling differences.

Each one of these visualizations follows on naturally from a meditation and is completed by the 'coming out' process of the same meditation (see chapter on Centering and Meditation). However, the visualizations in this chapter can also be used in isolation (as suggested above), without the complete meditation process, when necessary.

PERCEPTION

Prior to this visualization it is helpful to look at the picture on p.81 together. Experience the meaning of the word perception by looking at the young lady and then the old lady in the same picture. You can also study an object from two different angles, noting the difference in your perception from one angle

Figure 15.

to another. Or; how many ways can you look at a flower? From beneath the petals, from above, at eye level or at an angle. In the dark or in sunlight, wet and soggy with filthy petals or just fresh with morning dew and speckled with tiny grains of soil?

See before you now a clearing in nature. It can be any way you want it to be. . . . On the ground are a few scattered leaves, freshly fallen, green and shiny. You pick one up. Hold it between your fingers and feel the texture. How does the top of the leaf feel? Does it feel different underneath? Is it rough or smooth?. . . . Wet or dry?. . . . Now hold it up to your face and smell it. . . . Now study the surface. . . . Does the coloring

vary. . . . or is it the same green all over? Hold it at different
angles. . . . see from which angle it looks the prettiest. . . . Now
lay it down on the ground again. I want you to sit down next
to your leaf and for a moment, focus all your attention on your
heart. . . . Now begin to feel yourself getting smaller. . . . smaller
and smaller until you can fit inside your own heart. Smaller
and smaller until you are smaller than your leaf. Now I want
you to climb onto your leaf and sit down. . . . What does the
surface feel like now?. . . . How does it smell?. . . . How strong
is the color?. . . . Be on your leaf for a while and really enjoy
the feeling of being there. . . . You can move around on the leaf
if you want. . . . Now slide or jump off the leaf, landing on the
soft ground beneath you. You crawl underneath the leaf, lie
down and pull it over you like a blanket. Make yourself very
comfortable. . . . Feel the leaf against your skin. Feel the
temperature of the leaf. . . . however warm or cool, it is just
right for you. Feel yourself becoming that perfect temperature.
. . . Gradually feel yourself becoming the leaf. . . . Now you
are the leaf. How does it feel to be a leaf?. . . . How does it feel
to be green?. . . . How does it feel to have the leafy texture?. . . .
Feel what it is like to *be* a leaf for a while. . . . Enjoy it. . . .
(*pause*). . . . Now gradually feel yourself becoming yourself
again. . . . Gradually you return to your normal size. . . . Now
thank the leaf for letting you hold it, be on it and for letting
you *be* the leaf for a while. . . . Now focus your attention on
your heart again. . . . (*Return to the appropriate section of the
meditation process.*)

THE HEART

For this visualization it helps to sit facing each other.

Bring all your attention to your heart. Feel the rhythm of your
heartbeat. Listen closely and see if you can feel a peace, a deep
stillness, deep inside of you. Feel the peace within your heart.
. . . feel your heart fill with peace. . . . and with love. Your heart
is brimming over.
    Now send some of that love to the person facing you. . . .

Feel the love going from your heart to theirs. . . . Now feel their love coming back to you. . . . Now send some love to a friend or a family member. . . . Feel the love going from your heart to theirs. . . . Now feel their love coming back to you. . . . Feel the warmth within you. . . . Feel the peace. . . . Now send some love to ———— (*name a person with whom your child is experiencing conflict*). Feel the love going from your heart to theirs. . . . Send the love freely and easily and generously. . . . See if you can feel warmth and a sense of peace within you. . . . Now feel their love coming back to you. . . . Now hold onto that feeling of peace and love in your heart. . . . (*pause*). . . . Keep your attention focused on your heart. Listen to your heartbeat again. . . . (*Return to the appropriate section of the meditation process.*)

BE ANOTHER

Focus your attention on your heart and think for a moment of someone or something you love. Enjoy the good feeling it gives you. Stay with that feeling for a moment. . . . (*pause*). . . . Feel the love spreading out from your heart and filling your entire body. . . . and the room around you. . . . Now holding onto that feeling in your heart, I want you to imagine that you are someone else. . . . someone that you like and admire. . . . an older child at your school maybe? It can be anyone you like. Just imagine being that person. . . . (*pause*). . . . Now imagine seeing ———— (*name the person with whom your child is experiencing conflict*) through the eyes of the person you now are. Place ———— before you, in the center of this room. Keep holding on to the good and loving feeling in your heart as you look at ———— What do you see? As the person you now are, feeling love in your heart, what do you see?. . . . (pause). . . . Does ———— appear different?. . . . How would you *now* respond to ———— ?. . . . Holding on to the feeling of love, I want you to be yourself again. Now send some of all that love in your heart to ———— Send it freely, easily and generously. . . . See if you don't now feel a little different towards ———— Keep your attention focused on your heart. . . . Hold on to that feeling of love. . . . (*Return to the appropriate section of the meditation process.*)

It can be helpful, after these visualizations, to talk about what your child saw differently and whether he or she feels different. You may need to do the visualization a few times but in my experience, perseverance will reap rewards!

For the very young, the visualization 'Clouds of Perception' (see chapter Creating a Garden) can be appropriate when introducing the concept of perception and of 'seeing things from another point of view'.

 *Global Awareness*

Increasing global awareness and the sense of oneness with all creation is more important now than ever before. Most children today are very aware of this and creative visualization can assist them in experiencing being part of a greater whole.

The images used in these visualizations are suitable for all ages, although you can adapt the language to suit the age and mentality of your child if necessary.

Each one of the visualizations follows on naturally from a meditation and is completed by the 'coming out' process of the same meditation (see chapter on Centering and Meditation).

THE SEED

See before you a beautiful place in nature. . . . see a beautiful field or garden in your place of nature. . . . seat yourself on the ground in your field or garden. . . . feel the cool soft grass beneath you. . . . Smell the fresh scent of the grass. . . . Open the palm of your hand and see before you a tiny seed, right there in the palm of your hand. Now I want you to plant the seed in the ground in front of you. Take your time planting it and watering it as the sun shines down upon you. . . . Focus your attention on your heart and feel the love there in your heart. Send some of that love to the seed you have planted. . . . Imagine waves of love going from your heart to the seed in the ground. For each wave you send, imagine the seed growing in the ground until it peers through the soft dark earth. As you send waves of love, see it growing until it is a long green stalk with a small bud at its tip. Gradually this bud opens out into a beautiful white flower. . . . Gently you touch the soft petals.

How does this make you feel? Now feel yourself beginning to grow smaller. . . . smaller and smaller and smaller until you are small enough to fit inside the flower. . . . Crawl inside the flower now and make yourself comfortable between the petals. Feel how soft they are against your skin. Smell the strong, sweet fragrance of the flower, all around you. Enjoy being within this flower. . . . gradually become part of the flower. . . . (*pause*). . . . Now slowly feel yourself coming out of the flower and returning to your normal size and self. Gently touch the flower and know that you are part of it and of all of nature. . . . (*Return to the appropriate section of the meditation process.*)

THE TREE

See before you a beautiful place in nature. . . . See a clearing in your place in nature and put yourself in that clearing. . . . Imagine now that you are a tree. . . .

You can refer now to the Be A Tree exercise in the chapter Releasing Restrictions or to the yoga exercise The Tree in the chapter Creative Movement, if you feel this might help your child to experience the visualization within his or her body.

You are a tall tree with a strong trunk and many, many leafy branches. Although your branches may sway in the light breeze, they are so thick with leaves that they are a perfect place for any animal, bird or insect that needs shelter. Notice the sound of rustling leaves all around you and the feeling of being firmly planted in the ground. . . . Notice a few birds landing on your branches, building nests and singing their birdsong around you. . . . How does that feel? . . . . Now notice an animal or two. . . . maybe a lamb or a horse or a rabbit, sheltering under your branches and resting by your trunk. . . . How does that feel? . . . . What does it feel like to be this tree? . . . (*pause*). . . . Now bring your attention to your heart, feeling all the love you have there for the trees and the birds and the animals. Send some of that love out to all the trees and creatures of the world. . . . Now gradually come back to being yourself again. . . . keeping that feeling of love in your heart. . . . Know that you are part of all of nature. . . . (*Return to the appropriate section of the meditation process.*)

THE GLOBE

See before you a stream of light going into your heart. Feel your heart filling up with light and love. Now feel the light filling up your entire body. . . . Now the area around your body, and the room around you. . . . The light is filling up the building you are in, the town and then the whole country. . . . Feel the light that is streaming through your heart, fill the whole world, covering all of the globe with light and love. . . . Now feel yourself so filled with light and love that you begin to expand. Feel yourself growing larger and larger. . . . and the world becoming smaller and smaller in comparison. . . . Soon you are so large that you find yourself larger than an entire country. . . . any country you care to think of. . . . Now you find yourself floating just above this country, covering the whole country. . . . The light is still streaming through your heart. . . . I want you now to send some of all that love you have in your heart. . . . I want you to send it to all the people and creatures in that country. . . . Send the love and the light all over the country so that everyone there feels that they are bathing in bright loving sunlight. See all the people and the creatures in your country turn their faces towards the loving sunlight. . . . See them all feeling the peace and love you are sending. . . . (*pause*). . . . Now gradually return to your normal size. . . . still feeling the love and peace in your heart. . . . Know that you can *fill* the world with the love in your heart. . . . (*Return to the appropriate section of the meditation process.*)

THE STARS

See before you the moon in a deep blue night sky. . . . See a moonbeam streaming down and shining onto the ground in

front of you. . . . Now I want you to step into the moonbeam.
. . . As you stand there surrounded by moonlight, you feel the
energy of the moon pulling you upwards. You begin to rise.
. . . up, up. . . . soon you are soaring up, up, up through the
moonbeam. . . . up into the night sky. . . . Now you are flying.
. . . you leave the moonbeam behind you and fly across the
night sky. . . . There are stars all around you, sparkling like
diamonds. . . . Feel yourself opening your arms and parting the
stars as you soar through the air. . . . (*pause*). . . . Feel a light
shining in your heart. . . . sparkling like the stars around you.
. . . Feel all the love in your heart and send some of that love
to the stars and to the universe as you glide along, effortlessly
through the atmosphere. . . . Feel that you are one with the
stars and the sky around you. . . . (*pause*). . . . Now you see
your moonbeam in the distance. . . . you approach it and enter
the beautiful moonlight. . . . Gradually you return to Earth
through the moonbeam. . . . Feel the sparkling love in your
heart and *know* that you are part of the universe. . . . (*Return
to the appropriate section of the meditation process.*)

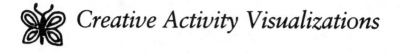 *Creative Activity Visualizations*

Focusing a visualization on the activity to follow can greatly enhance the quality of the activity and what is achieved with it. The more central the activity, the more of an enhancement the visualization can be. In my twenty years of using visualization when working with children I have always had one motto; If you can see yourself doing it, you can do it! This motto has not failed me yet! The power of the imagination is indeed great when it comes to the performance of an activity or taking action. In my experience it is often how we *imagine* ourselves achieving something that determines whether or not – and in what way – we will achieve it! Let me give you a brief example. If you place a plank on the carpet of your living room floor and ask anyone to balance along it, chances are that they will manage this perfectly well. If, however, you place the plank between two tall trees, several feet above asphalted ground, whoever you ask to balance across it will probably have second thoughts – even if they managed very well when the plank was on your carpet! This is because they begin to *imagine* what may happen if they fall off. If they do attempt to walk the plank between the trees, their balance will probably be considerably reduced – also due to their imagination.

If we can show our children how to use their imagination and visualization abilities for the purpose of stretching themselves and helping them to achieve, instead of supporting fear, the quality of their lives can only be improved!

Using focused and creative visualization for the purpose of enhancing an activity can take several forms, depending on the experience you wish to motivate:

1. The experience of being the *essence* of the activity.

2. The experience of being the *instrument* of the activity.
3. The experience of *being* the activity.
4. The experience of *creating* the activity.

All of the above are helpful to increase enjoyment, quality of understanding and performance, and achievement levels. I have chosen one visualization for each purpose of experience. Using these as guidelines, you can create your own visualizations both to suit an activity you and your child have chosen, and to give the experience you believe to be most appropriate for your child, within the activity.

Each one of the visualizations follows on naturally from a meditation and is completed by the 'coming out' process of the same meditation (see chapter on Centering and Meditation).

Visualizations such as these *can* be created and used independently of your sessions, for example prior to a soccer game, a ballet class or a music lesson.

EARTH

Experiencing the *essence* of the activity
Activity to follow; gardening or re-potting a plant.

See before you a plant (*this can be the plant you are planning to re-pot or whatever you are to plant in the garden*). Notice how green the leaves are. Feel the texture of the leaves and smell their scent. . . . Now focus your attention on your heart for a moment. . . . Think of something you love and then think of your plant. . . . and how beautiful it is. Enjoy the good feeling these thoughts give you. . . . Now feel yourself beginning to grow small. . . . smaller and smaller until you can sit on one of the leaves of your plant. How does the leaf feel now? . . . . Begin to slide down the leaf. . . . Now hold onto the stalk and slowly slide down the stalk, getting smaller and smaller until you land on the earth and are merely the size of a small particle of earth. . . . You are now part of the earth. Feel yourself going into the earth. . . . you are one with the earth. . . . Feel the temperature. . . . the texture. . . . the smell. . . . Feel the soil and the rocks and the clay and every particle of earth as part of you. . . . (*pause*). . . . A spade is now gently digging around the base of the plant. Feel yourself and the soil around you being shifted. . . . the roots of the plant loosening underneath you. . . . You are lifted up on the spade together with the plant and all the earth, and you are placed in new earth. Feel yourself blending with the new soil. . . . being gently tossed about. . . . and then watered. You become moist and cool. . . . You are settling in now. . . . enjoy it. . . . Now gradually come up out of the earth, up along the stalk and up onto the leaf. . . . and return to your normal self and size. . . . Feel love in your heart for the plant and for the earth, knowing you are one with them both. . . . Thank them for being there for you. . . . (*Return to the appropriate section of the meditation process.*)

AIR

Experiencing the *instrument* of the activity
Activity to follow; flying a kite

See before you a wide open space in nature, and at your feet your very own kite. Notice the material the kite is made of. . . . the colors and the pattern. . . . Now focus your attention on your heart for a moment. . . . Think of something or someone you love. . . . and then think of your own special kite. . . . Enjoy the nice feeling these thoughts give you. . . . (*pause*). . . . Now feel yourself beginning to grow small. . . . smaller and smaller until you are the size of a pin and you are standing next to the edge of your kite. . . . Reach out and touch your kite. . . . What does the material of the kite feel like?. . . . What does the pattern of the kite look like from here?. . . . What colors do you see? . . . Climb up onto your kite and feel yourself becoming part of it. . . . Feel yourself being one with the material. . . . with the colors. . . . Now feel the kite slowly lifting off the ground. . . . gradually it rises. . . . higher and higher and higher until you are soaring through the air. . . . Feel yourself riding on the wind as it carries you along. . . . You are one with the air around you. . . . (*pause*). . . . You are soaring across the countryside,

over hills and valleys, rivers and forests, mountains and lakes.
. . . Now you begin to come down. . . . and then your kite-string
jerks and you soar up again. . . . You feel the wind become
gentler and slowly you begin to drift down towards the ground.
Feel the gentle breeze around you. . . . you are still riding on
the air as you drift down onto the ground landing softly. . . .
You gradually come out of and off the kite and return to your
normal self and size. . . . (*pause*). . . . Bring your attention to
your heart and feel the love you have there for the wind, the
air and this exciting adventure you have had. . . . and for your
kite for sharing it with you. . . . Thank them all. . . . (*Return
to the appropriate section of the meditation process.*)

WATER

Experiencing *being* the activity
Activity to follow; swimming

See before you a pool/lake/the sea (*choose whichever applies
to you*). The water is clear blue and the sun is shining overhead.
Dip your hands into the water and feel its softness. . . . Now
focus your attention on your heart for a moment. . . . Think
of something you love. . . . and think of the blue inviting water.
. . . Enjoy the warm feeling these thoughts give you. . . . Now
go into the water gradually. . . . feel the water against your
skin, lapping gently against your body. . . . Notice the temperature of the water. . . . Feel yourself becoming that
temperature. . . . Feel yourself floating in the water until you
feel as though you are one with the water. . . . Feel yourself
moving through the water now. . . . gracefully and effortlessly
gliding through the water. . . . Feel each stroke you take moving
you along with even greater ease. . . . Your rhythm of movement blends in with the movement of the water until it is
one rhythm. . . . Enjoy being totally in harmony with the
water. . . . (*pause*). . . . Flow with the water. . . . play with the
water. . . . enjoy the water. . . . Now gradually move towards
the edge of the water. . . . Come out of the water now. . . .
Bring your attention to your heart and feel the love you have

there for the water. . . . Thank the water for being there so generously. . . . (*Return to the appropriate section of the meditation process.*)

IMAGE

Experiencing *creating* the activity
Activity to follow; drawing or painting

See before you a large bare sheet of white paper. Next to it is a box full of colored pencils and paints. All the colors you could possibly want are in the box. . . . Focus your attention on your heart for a moment. . . . Think of something you love. . . . and think of the smooth paper in front of you and all the vibrant colored pencils and paints. . . . Enjoy the feeling these thoughts give you. . . . Now using your very favorite color, begin to draw or to paint. . . . whatever you want. . . . The pencil or brush moves freely in your hand, across the paper. . . . creating the most beautiful and perfect picture. . . . Notice the sound of the pencil or brush on the paper. . . . feel the texture of the paper and see the texture of the paint of colors. . . . Smell the scent of the paint or pencils as they move across the paper. . . . See yourself forming the exact lines and shapes you want. . . . See yourself creating the exact images you want to create. . . . See yourself using the perfect colors as your picture takes shape. . . . Enjoy the feeling of creating your perfect picture. . . . (*pause*). . . . Your picture is complete. . . . Step back and observe it. . . . Feel the love in your heart. . . . give some of all that love in your heart to yourself. . . . and to your picture. . . . Thank the paper, pencils and paint for being there for you to use. . . . (*Return to the appropriate section of the meditation process.*)

PART FOUR

Activities

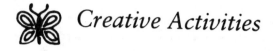 # Creative Activities

A creative activity following creative visualization will direct the energy accumulated during meditation, and facilitate the grounding of your child (and yourself!). It will also help to create a balance between the inner and the outer worlds, linking activity with centeredness and inner wisdom.

You can choose whether to make this connection consciously and clearly – by associating the visualization with the activity – or to let the subconscious absorb the link, leaving your child to make the connection in his or her own time and way. Both methods are equally valuable and can be used alternately and in accordance with your child's and family's needs. If you are unsure as to which one to use, follow your intuition!

Be sure to choose your activity beforehand and make any preparations necessary, so as not to disrupt the process. The following are some suggestions for activities and creative outlets to follow creative visualization.

Gardening: You can do this on a small or a grand scale, from potting houseplants and growing cress to planting a whole vegetable garden. If the weather permits you may like to do the entire session outside. In my experience, children love meditating and doing creative visualization outdoors.

Swimming: It is preferable if this is done in a river or the sea but if this is not possible, try to choose a quiet time at your local pool. You can use this activity to familiarize your child with the water if there is any apprehension. However, it is not advisable to use this as a swimming 'lesson'. Your child should be able to do the basic strokes and to stay afloat in the water if he or she is to truly benefit from swimming after visualizing. If you are swimming by the sea or a lake, you may wish to do the entire session in the open air. If you have to travel to a pool, see if you can encourage your child to recreate any appropriate sensations from the visualization as you move in the water. This will help to bridge the time gap caused by the travel.

Drawing/Painting: This can also be done outside, weather permitting. Your child may wish to draw or paint what they saw in their meditation. Eventually however, it is advisable to draw or paint what they see (especially if you are outside) and add what they saw in their meditation and visualization. The finished picture then becomes reality and fantasy intertwined and can be an important exercise in achieving balance.

Batik or Tie-Dye: It is advisable to try this yourself before doing it with children. Be sure to let your child create his or her own design freely. You can enhance the experience by bringing the awareness to the color of the dye, the texture of the material, the feel of the water against the skin, the smell of the dye and all the various sounds involved.

Clay Modelling or Plasticine: As this can be rather messy, be sure you have plenty of time to clean up afterwards to insure that the activity is not rushed. Encourage your child to create something from their meditation and visualization. As with the drawing, they can eventually combine images of what they see in their physical reality with what they have seen in their meditation and visualization, giving them another tool for experiencing balance.

Music: If you and your child play musical instruments, you can improvise on these together or alternatively compose a tune together. If your child has written a poem, you may like to put this to music. You can also create rhythms to songs, using household articles such as a bottle and a spoon (hit the bottle with the spoon in rhythm – but not too hard!) or a wooden spoon and a grater (scrape it up and down in rhythm) or two spoons and an old washboard (scrape it up and down and beat it like a drum). You can use old bicycle bells, fill tins with dried peas and use them as maracas or hit two pieces of wood together. The favorite, however, is usually the beating of pots and pans with spoons! Whichever way you choose, making music together can enhance a sense of family togetherness as well as being mutually creative.

Dancing: You may have danced or done creative movement at the beginning of the session and wish to continue with this as a creative activity. If so, it is advisable to use music that 'moves' you both. Try to use music that is changeable, such as an overture, as this encourages the expression of all aspects of the music. Improvise and dance freely to the music or create your own dances together.

Kino Visualization: You may occasionally like to do more image-body movement (see chapter on Kino Visualization) as a creative activity. If so, I suggest that you do this to music, preferably music that both you and your child enjoy. You can elaborate on the exercises and processes in the chapter on Kino Visualization and eventually create your own.

Shadow Dancing: Again, choose a piece of music that inspires you both to move. Stand opposite each other (if you are more than two, stand in pairs). Choose one to be the instigator. As that person moves, the other must respond or follow the movement with their own, either in shadow or partner fashion. After a while, change roles. Observe and enjoy the many different variations and relationships that unfold. Give this activity time to develop.

Writing: This is usually more appropriate for slightly older children. Write, and let your child write short accounts, poems or essays of the meditation and visualization experience. You can eventually write a short story that unfolds within or from the visualization. Share your writings with each other (without judgement) if you both feel comfortable doing so.

Album: You may like to keep an album each of your meditation and visualization processes. In this album, you can draw, write, stick photos or your favorite pictures cut out from magazines and generally do whatever you feel will support and express your visualizations, aims and goals.

Double Drawing: Spread a large sheet of paper on the floor and place yourself and your child on either side of it. Begin to draw – in an improvised fashion – on either side of the paper. Discuss the experience of your meditation and visualization process that day, as you draw. You can also play music in the background to keep the atmosphere as casual and relaxed as possible. Observe at what point the drawings fuse and how decisions are made to fuse the drawings. How do they finally become one drawing?

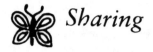 *Sharing*

When you have completed the meditation and creative visualization process – and your creative activity – it can be of great value to share some of the experiences you had during these processes. Although most children (and adults!) enjoy such sharing, it is important that this is a voluntary process. If your child does not wish to share one day, do not pressure him or her. Also, try to remember not to judge anything that is shared, in any way.

Sharing can be done in several ways. In my experience a certain structure or method is needed in order for everyone to benefit equally. Structure can also contribute to joint family or group benefits being derived, such as improved communication.

The following are some methods of sharing that I have found to be both beneficial and enjoyable. Whichever one you choose, be sure you leave enough time to complete it.

1. *Heart to Heart:* This is for two people only and is especially beneficial when you have previously done a meditation where all awareness is focused on the heart and on feeling love (see chapter on Centering and Meditation). When sharing Heart to Heart, one person speaks, sharing one experience in as much detail as possible. The other person listens while *feeling* love and sending love from their heart to the heart of the speaker, continuously. When the sharing is complete, the listener repeats – in his or her own words – all that has been shared. When this is concluded, change roles and repeat the whole process. Try to retain the feeling of love and keep sending this love to the other person throughout the process.

2. *Crystal:* This method is appropriate if someone is unsure of whether they wish to share, or if anyone for some reason may wish to share more than once. It can also be used to improve listening abilities. Have everyone seated in a circle or, if you are just two, facing each other. Place a crystal in the centre of the circle – I like to use a Rose Quartz as it represents love, but any crystal will do. Whoever wishes to share picks up the crystal and holds it as long as they are speaking. When their sharing is concluded they place the crystal back in the centre of the circle for whoever then wishes to pick it up and speak. *Only* the person holding the crystal is allowed to speak and those who are not speaking give him or her their complete attention.

3. *Round Robin:* This is a method best suited for a group of three or more. Everyone sits in a circle and one person shares their experience for a limited time period. The person on his or her right then follows with their own sharing – and so on until everyone in the circle has shared their experiences. Each person should share as much or as little as they wish and be allowed to speak freely, without any interruptions. It is important that everyone listens attentively to each other, until it is their turn to share.

Remember – in all the above three processes (or any other process of listening and sharing);

1. *Do not interrupt.*
2. *Do not judge.*
3. *Listen with love and compassion.*

 *Outflowing*

Outflowing is important for enhancing the sense of being part of a greater whole – a significant and valued way to conclude your session of creative visualization!

The following are some simple processes for outflowing that can be used with all ages.

Love Net:

For a group of three or more. Sit in a circle and take a few deep breaths together. 'Lead' the breathing.

Feel the rhythm of the breathing. In (breathe in) and out (breathe out). In (breathe in) and out (breathe out). Feel how your breathing is in rhythm with everyone in the room. . . . Now listen to your heartbeat. Imagine or feel that your heartbeat is in rhythm with everyone in the room. . . . feel all the heartbeats in rhythm. . . . beating together. . . . Now keeping the awareness in your heart, think about something or someone that makes you feel love. . . . Feel the love in your heart. . . . Now imagine a thread of beautiful warm pink light shining out of your heart and into the heart of the person on your left. . . . Now imagine another thread of beautiful warm pink light shining out of your heart and into the heart of the person on your right. . . . Now imagine another thread of beautiful warm pink light shining out of your heart and into the heart of the person sitting opposite you. . . . (*Repeat this until everyone has sent light from their heart to everyone else in the circle*). . . . Now send some of all that love you have in your heart, through the beautiful pink threads of light to the hearts of everyone in the circle. . . . Feel the love flowing. . . . out from your heart and into your heart. . . . Now bring your attention back to your breathing. . . . feel the slow relaxed rhythm of your breathing blend with everyone else in the circle. . . . Become aware of the room around you and when you are ready, open your eyes!

Universal Love:

This can be done with one or more. Sit comfortably and close your eyes.

Now take a few deep breaths until you feel relaxed and comfortable. . . . Now take a deep breath and feel the energy of the universe through the crown of your head. Feel it going down to your heart and filling your heart with love. . . . Now release it out into the universe, through your heart. Breathe in again, breathing in universal love and energy through the crown of your head and out through your heart. Again. . . . breathe in universal love, energy and wisdom. . . . in through the crown of your head and out through your heart. . . . Feel your body filling up with universal love. . . . feel the space around your body fill up with universal love. . . . As you breathe in and out, feel the whole room you are in fill up with universal love, energy and wisdom. . . . Feel the entire building fill up with universal love. . . . Breathe in and out and feel the area around your building fill with universal love, energy and wisdom. . . . Feel the town filling up. . . . and then the entire country. . . . filled with universal love, energy and wisdom. Breathe in through the crown of your head and out through your heart and feel the entire continent fill with universal love. . . . Feel it spreading across the whole world. . . . Now feel the universal love, energy and wisdom completely filling the universe. . . . feel the oneness, the love, the wisdom and the energy. . . . and send out love and healing energy to all the people in this room. . . . to all the people in this country and to all the people in the whole world. . . . to situations and to anywhere you feel it is needed. . . . Everything is connected. . . . Now bring your attention back to your breathing. . . . Feel the slow relaxed rhythm of your breathing blending with everyone else in the room. . . . Become aware of the room around you and when you are ready, open your eyes. . . .

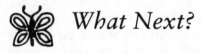 *What Next?*

Having tried all the processes in this book and found the ones that suit you and your child or children best, you may wish to explore the concept of creative visualization further. You may have already become aware – either through your own personal experience or through your child's – of the incredible possibilities that open up when you use creative visualization actively in your lives.

Personally I have explored it – and continue to explore it – with ever increasing wonder and joy, constantly discovering new depths and dimensions to its power. Even more wondrous is the new level visualization and the mind can reach when empowered by the heart. With the engagement of the heart, an amplification is achieved that gives the image or visualization experience additional powers of manifestation.

Should you also wish to explore further – and I strongly recommend you do – there are many wonderful books written for adults about creative visualization. I have listed some of my favorites in the recommended reading list at the back of this book. As for heart power, although an awareness of the power of love is as old as mankind, little or no attention has been paid to any formal research or scientific exploration of this wonder until quite recently. The Institute of HeartMath in California is currently doing extensive research into the power of the heart and how loving and caring feelings affect us and our health. They have published some excellent books on the subject – you can find their address in the back of this book.

Creative visualization works as well as it does because it can function on all levels; Mental, physical, emotional and spiritual. I truly hope this book has awakened your – and your child's – curiosity enough to encourage further exploration of these and the more subtle levels of creative visualization.

May your child's imagination – and indeed your own – be a 'force' that both enriches and empowers your lives.

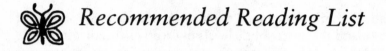# Recommended Reading List

For Children

The Crystal Lady by Deborah Rozman PhD, Planetary Publications, 1991.
An enchanting story book for age 5 and up, introducing children to the magical world of the heart. Children love the illustrations!

Snow Ghosts by Christopher Gilmore, Atma Ents, 1990.
A delightful fable, also available on cassette. For all ages.

Spiritual Teachings for Children by Jenny Dent, White Eagle Publishing Trust, 1982.
A series of 4 books filled with games, projects and meditations for children of all ages.

Every Day Can Feel Like Christmas by Paula Elliot, Planetary Publications, 1992.
A story and color book that teaches children that every day *can* feel like Christmas. Age 3 and up.

50 Simple Things Kids Can Do to Save the Earth by John Javna, The EarthWorks Group, 1990.
A great book full of experiments, facts and exciting things to do for children—and adults! This book can give children the confidence and the sense that they have the power to make a difference. Many of these activities can be used as Creative Activities within sessions of Creative Visualization.

Teen Self Discovery by Doc Lew Childre, Planetary Publications, 1992.
A book written for (American) teenagers, about self-esteem, inner security and 'growing up on the inside'. Written in teenage language, this book does an excellent job of introducing teenagers to their feelings and to the 'How To's' of building a positive self-image.

For Children and Parents

Meditation For Children by Deborah Rozman PhD, Planetary Publications, 1989.
A classic parenting bestseller which gives parents step-by-step instructions to help children relate to life with new confidence and joy.

Meditating With Children by Deborah Rozman PhD, Planetary Publications, 1975.
Meditation exercises for children including lesson plans for children ages pre-school to 8th grade. Cassette also available.

Joy in the Classroom by Stephanie Herzog, Planetary Publications, 1982.
A refreshing straight-from-the-heart book for parents as well as teachers. Simple but powerful processes that unlock children's creativity and produce break-throughs in their verbal, artistic and written expression.

Notes to my Children – A Simplified Metaphysics by Ken Carey, UniSun, 1982.
Another classic, this book tells many parables designed to awaken and nourish the child spirit in all.

For Parents and Other Adults

Creative Visualization by Shakti Gawain, New World Library, 1978.
The classic best seller on creative visualization. (A workbook is also available.) A clear and practical guide.

Life Choices and Life Changes Through Imagework by Dina Glouberman, Mandala, 1987.
Creative visualization as it is actually used in therapy and counselling – although the author calls it imagework.

I See Myself in Perfect Health by David Lawson, Healing Workshops Press, 1990.
Creative visualization for health; ideas to fire your imagination for personal healing or just enhanced health.

The Silva Mind Control Method by Jose Silva and Philip Miele, Simon and Schuster, 1977.
Techniques and practices in creative visualization by one of the leading pioneers in this area.

Meditations by Shakti Gawain, New World Library, 1991.
Popular meditations and visualizations, also available on cassette.

The Possible Human by Jean Houston, Tarcher, 1982.
A book to read and do! Many wonderful exercises in Body-Image work; Jean Houston is a pioneer in this field.

Freeze Frame by Doc Lew Childre, Planetary Publications, 1994. A practical and timely book for individual and family stress management through the heart.

Imagineering for Health by Serge King, Quest, 1981. An excellent book on self-healing through the use of the mind and the imagination.

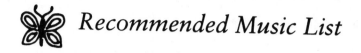 *Recommended Music List*

FOR CREATIVE VISUALIZATION SESSIONS

Tension Release (shaking)

Spirit of the Rainforest by Terry Oldfield, New World Cassettes, 1990.

Dance the Devil Away by Outback, Rykodisc, 1991.

Or any good African drumming and percussion tape.

Improvised Dance

The Four Seasons (Vivaldi) with Nigel Kennedy, EMI, 1987.

Appalachian Spring (Copeland) with the Detroit Symphony Orchestra, Decca, 1986.

Variations (Andrew Lloyd Webber with Julian Lloyd Webber), MCA Records, 1978.

On Your Toes Rodgers and Hart Original Soundtrack, 1983. Polygram, 1983. (When using this and other musicals, use the instrumental – non-vocal – selections whenever possible.)

Cats by Andrew Lloyd Webber, Polydor, 1981.

Mime Dancing

Soil Festivities Vangelis, Polydor, 1984.

Electric Cafe Kraftwerk, EMI, 1986.

Blue Tango Symphonic Pops Leroy Andersen, WDR, 1989.

Breathing music / sound effects

An Island Called Paradise by David Sun, New World Cassettes, 1984.

Whales & Sounds of the Sea (three dimensional environmental sounds with subliminals), New World Cassettes, 1988.

Ocean Waves (with subliminals), New World Cassettes, 1988.

Ocean Waves at Sunset, New World Cassettes, 1992.

Calming music for meditations and visualizations

Harmony by David Sun, New World Cassettes, 1992.

The Healing Harp with Patricia Spero, New World Cassettes, 1990.

The Calmer Panorama by Tim Wheater, Warner Bros. Music, 1986.

Radiance by Steve Halpern, Sound Rx, 1989.

Music from the Pleiades by Gerald Jay Markoe, Astro Music, 1989.

The Enchanted Forest by David Sun, New World Cassettes, 1990.

Sea Green by Sarah Wexel, New World Cassettes, 1990.

Tapes for children

Peter and the Wolf with the Royal Philharmonic Orchestra. Narrated by Sean Connery, Contour, 1966.
(Act it out with improvised dance and mime!)

Buddy Bubbles. Games for a Child's Heart (ages 2–8), Planetary Publications, 1992.

Useful Addresses

The Institute of HeartMath
PO Box 1463
Boulder Creek
California 95006
USA

Planetary Publications
PO Box 66
Boulder Creek
California 95006
USA

White Eagle Lodge Children's Group
White Eagle Publishing Trust
New Lands
Liss
Hampshire GU33 7HY
England

The Silva Method International
1110 Cedar Avenue
Laredo
Texas 78040
USA

The Kids' Earth Works Group
1400 Shattuck Avenue, #25
Berkeley
California 94709
USA

Development Education Project
(Resources for Teachers and Families)
801 Wilmslow Road
Didsbury
Manchester M20 2QR
England